Tales
from the
Triple Crown

Tales
from the
Triple Crown

STEVE
HASKIN

Lexington, Kentucky

ECLIPSE
PRESS

Library of Congress Control Number: 2008920355

ISBN: 978-1-58150-184-1

Printed in the United States
First Edition: 2008

a division of
Blood-Horse Publications
PUBLISHERS SINCE 1916

Contents

Introduction

This is not a history of the Triple Crown. You will find very few facts and figures or insightful analysis. The earliest reference, in fact, is 1971. The book is intended to be a compilation of human-interest stories, most seen through my eyes, first as national correspondent for the *Daily Racing Form* and then as senior correspondent for *The Blood-Horse* since 1999.

Every story since 1992 is based on my experience as a first-hand observer and journalist covering the three events. I have tried not to be too intrusive, but on several occasions I feel my observations and my involvement add to the story. It is on those occasions that I injected myself into the chapter. Prior to 1991 are stories I have either come across after the fact or observed as a freelance writer and, in one case, a photographer.

As the originator of "Derby Watch" and the "Road

to the Kentucky Derby" columns, as well as the daily Preakness and Belmont reports, I have had the privilege of being close to many horsemen leading up to and through the Triple Crown and have saved all my notes taken the past sixteen years. From those notes, along with articles and features I have written, I have been able to put together a collection of stories I think capture the excitement and human drama of the Triple Crown. These stories are about the horses and the horsemen, and I hope they will provide a behind-the-scenes look at the Triple Crown most people normally do not get a chance to see or hear about.

Not all the featured horses are winners. Many have already faded into the furthest regions of our memory. But that doesn't make their stories any less compelling. A good number of the horsemen mentioned are Hall of Famers, and some, such as Bob Baffert, show up in more than one chapter. Others are lesser known, but for one year they commanded the headlines. There is nothing in racing as bright as the Triple Crown spotlight, and often the transient visitors who bask in it provide the best stories.

There will be many recognizable subjects, such as Charlie Whittingham, D. Wayne Lukas, Baffert, Angel Cordero Jr., Spectacular Bid, Silver Charm, Unbridled's Song, and Smarty Jones, just to name a few, and some not so recognizable names, such as Nancy Alberts, Andy Durnin, Hanne Jorgensen, Mick Jenner, Magic Weisner, and Irgun.

This book could have been titled *Five Weeks Every Spring*, as each year, from the first Saturday in May to early June, new and old names and faces enter our psyche, some for just a short while. Others remain forever. And it is to those who have provided everlasting memories that this book is dedicated.

Steve Haskin
Hamilton Square, New Jersey

1

·················

The One and Only Bid
(1979)

P eople are always asking me who is the greatest horse I've ever seen. I tell them Secretariat and Damascus had the most incredible three-year-old campaigns, and Dr. Fager, in 1968, was the greatest horse that ever set foot on an American racetrack. But over the course of a career — at ages two, three, and four — Spectacular Bid was the greatest horse I have ever seen, and he was the one horse who didn't sweep the Triple Crown who should have.

Following his death in 2003, I wrote a tribute to The Bid. This chapter will include portions of that tribute, as well as glimpses of his journey through the Triple Crown.

Spectacular Bid's trainer, Buddy Delp, once called him "the greatest horse to ever look through a bridle." People either laughed at his comment or paid no attention to the rantings of this Maryland hardboot.

There have been better-looking horses. There have been better-moving horses and better-bred horses. But The Bid had one quality that separated him from the others — he could do everything. He won grade I stakes on the lead, and he won coming from ten lengths back. He ran seven furlongs in a near-world-record 1:20 flat and 1¼ miles in an American record 1:57⅘, a time that has not been equaled on dirt in twenty-eight years. He broke seven track records and equaled another, and he did it at ages two, three, and four. As a two-year-old, he won the World's Playground Stakes at Atlantic City by fifteen lengths, running the seven furlongs over a dead racetrack eased up in an astounding 1:20⅘.

He won at fifteen different racetracks in nine different states and carried 130 pounds or more to victory five times. To demonstrate his dominance, and the respect the public had for him, he was sent off at odds of 1-20 — that's 1-20 — an unheard of nine times, and 1-10 five times. Beginning with the World's Playground, he won twenty-four of twenty-six starts, rattling off twelve-race and ten-race winning streaks while facing such classy grade I winners as Flying Paster, General Assembly, Coastal, Glorious Song, Cox's Ridge, and Golden Act. Interrupting those winning streaks were defeats at 1½ miles — in the Belmont, when he stepped on a safety pin that morning, almost losing his foot after a bad infection set in, and in the Jockey Club Gold Cup, when he was beaten by Hall of Famer Affirmed after a virus forced him to miss his prep in the Woodward Stakes.

But The Bid's appeal went far beyond statistics. As a four-year-old, his coat lightened, making him a ghostly figure as he hurtled down one stretch after another in isolated splendor. With his head held high and his powerful legs stretching across the racing universe, not only did he go undefeated in nine starts in 1980, he did so without a horse in front of him from the eighth pole to the wire.

My wife, Joan, and I have always felt a kinship with The Bid. He was a part of our early life together, before we were married, and his passing in 2003 unleashed a flood of memories, especially ones surrounding his 1979 Triple Crown bid.

A week before Joan started working as public relations coordinator for the New York Racing Association, we were hired as freelance photographers by a weekly racing publication, for which I had been writing part time, to cover the Preakness Stakes.

Of course, all the talk was about Maryland hero Spectacular Bid, who had swept through his Kentucky Derby preps with ease and then handily defeated the swift General Assembly in the Kentucky Derby, with California sensation Flying Paster finishing out of the money.

Covering the Preakness was easy. All we had to do was hang around Spectacular Bid. Sharing the stakes barn with The Bid was future Hall of Famer Davona Dale, the great Calumet Farm filly who had already won four stakes that year, including the grade I Kentucky Oaks and Fantasy Stakes. The day before the Preakness, Davona Dale cruised home an easy winner of the Black-Eyed

Susan Stakes. She would go on to sweep New York's Filly Triple Crown — the Acorn, Mother Goose, and Coaching Club American Oaks.

A great photo opportunity presented itself Preakness morning when Spectacular Bid walked the shed after training. When he passed by Davona Dale's stall, she thrust her neck out and pinned her ears. The Bid stopped right in front of her stall, and with his eyes as big as saucers, he stared her down for several seconds before continuing. Next time around, there was Davona Dale's outstretched head, her ears again pinned back to her shoulders. And there was The Bid, stopping in his tracks and flashing the whites of his eyes at her. This routine would go on every time the colt passed by.

Earlier in the day we were able to get another great photo of The Bid as he came off the track. Walking back along the rail with his groom, Mo Hall, he began bucking and lashing out with his back legs. I was able to catch him with both hind legs well up off the ground. Hall, holding on for dear life, began hollering at him. "Damn, you're as crazy as the boss," he said, referring to the often-volatile Delp.

Later that afternoon I shot photos from inside the rail near the finish line while Joan found a spot on the outside rail. Together, we were able to record Spectacular Bid's dominating 5½-length victory, in which he missed the track record by one-fifth of a second.

History shows that Spectacular Bid was upset in the Belmont Stakes, finishing third behind Coastal and

Golden Act, two horses he had crushed every other time he faced them.

The morning before the Belmont, The Bid had breezed three furlongs in :35 and change. Following the work, Delp was sitting in the barn with several workers, including Hall. Delp looked at The Bid, who had his head out the door, and said in his typical cocky manner. "Well, boys, there he is. The Triple Crown is ours, without a doubt. All we have to do is lead him over there."

On Saturday morning Delp was driven to the track, arriving just before daylight. As soon as he got out of the limo, Hall came running over to him and said, "Boss, the horse is lame." Delp raced to the The Bid's stall and turned on the light. The horse was standing in the middle of the stall holding his left front leg in the air. Hall kneeled down and held the leg while Delp examined it. Sticking in the hoof a good half-inch was an open safety pin.

It seems that when The Bid had been fed at four o'clock that morning, Hall had inadvertently dropped a safety pin in the straw. Spectacular Bid was hungry and stomping for his food. It was a one-in-a-million shot, but his foot struck the safety pin, which was sticking straight up. He came down on it so hard he drove the pin well up into his foot. Hall had no idea what had happened. All he knew was that the horse was lame. He was so upset he didn't even bother to look at the foot. So, Bid had the pin in his foot for a good ninety minutes.

Delp eased it out slowly, and with it came a thin, brown fluid. There was no evidence of the entry wound because the bacteria the horse had picked up from the straw had sealed it off. Once the pin had been removed, The Bid appeared to be sound and started bouncing and playing around the barn, obviously happy to have this foreign object out of his foot. To help prevent infection, Delp packed the colt's foot with mud, Epsom salts, and vinegar, a mixture known as Bowie mud.

He then broke the news to owner Harry Meyerhoff and told him if the foot wasn't 100 percent sound when he returned in the afternoon, he would have to scratch the horse. When Delp arrived, The Bid seemed perfectly sound, so Delp kept the incident from the media. He felt that The Bid could win the Belmont even if he wasn't 100 percent, and the trainer remained upbeat all day. He did make one mistake, which he regretted until the day he died. Whenever he talked about it many years later, it still brought him to tears.

He was always convinced he should have left jockey Ron Franklin in the dark about the pin so the jockey would not have it on his mind during the race. Delp felt that Franklin just wanted to get the race over with and foolishly sent The Bid after an 85-1 shot on the lead with a mile still to run. Delp could tell The Bid was running in pain. His action was different, and he wasn't striding out comfortably. Coming into the stretch, The Bid, uncharacteristically, did not change leads, again indicating something was bothering him. Delp was tortured watching him, knowing he could have scratched him and didn't. But he truly had believed the horse could win anyway.

After the race Delp stood outside the test barn, drinking a bottle of beer, and said nothing to the press except that there were no excuses. All he wanted was to go see whether the horse was OK and get out of there. After returning to Maryland the following day, he told a few local reporters about the safety pin, and word quickly spread. Many people didn't believe Delp, saying he was just making excuses. They accused him of lying, which upset him only because the accusations brought his mother to tears.

But The Bid's problems were far from over. Delp called noted veterinarian Alex Harthill, who told him to tub the foot in warm water and Epsom salts twice a day, then apply a poultice to seal everything up. If it wasn't any better in a week, Harthill would fly up from Kentucky. The Bid appeared fine after a week, but on the eighth day, he was lame. Delp called Harthill and told him to get up there quickly.

After arriving, the veterinarian used a miniature plane-like instrument to remove a little bit of hoof at a time. He noticed a black spot deep in the hoof and bore into it with an electric drill. As soon as the drill penetrated the spot, a thick, black fluid spurted out as if he had struck oil. The foot was badly infected and needed immediate treatment.

Harthill looked up at Delp and said, "Hey, Bud, where are all those sonsabitches who called you a liar?"

Harthill told Delp if the foot had gone much longer

without being treated, the horse likely would have lost it, which in turn could have cost him his life.

Back in Kentucky, Harthill had blacksmith Jack Reynolds fly to Maryland to fit The Bid with a special piece of aluminum for his shoe to support and protect the foot. Delp fed the colt gelatin to toughen the hoof wall and medicated the coronet band to stimulate blood circulation and help the hoof grow back.

A little more than two months later, The Bid returned in an allowance race at Delaware Park with a new jockey, Bill Shoemaker, aboard and broke the track record, winning eased up by seventeen lengths. The Bid was back. His career would continue to skyrocket, taking him and Delp to new heights.

Eleven months after that allowance win, Joan and I watched from her Belmont Park office overlooking the finish line, as Spectacular Bid, his name already etched in history as one of the greats of all time, concluded his remarkable career with the first walkover in thirty-one years. Eight days later we were married.

Even The Bid's walkover in the Woodward Stakes was an amazing performance. The colt had been battling a sesamoid problem all year, and Delp told Shoemaker just to cruise around the track. Instead, The Bid wound up running the 1¼ miles in 2:02⅖, closing his last two quarters in an unbelievable :24⅕. Horses don't come home that fast in a hotly run race, never mind in a race against no one. The final time was faster than it took Hall of Famers Kelso and Buckpasser to win the Woodward.

Delp said he thought going in that The Bid likely had only one more race left in him, and he was not happy about Shoemaker's letting him run that fast in a walkover with the Jockey Club Gold Cup coming up. Shortly after the race Delp discovered The Bid had aggravated his sesamoid again, and he was forced to scratch him from the Gold Cup. That marked the end of Spectacular's Bid remarkable career. With no other major races left for him, he was retired to Claiborne Farm in Paris, Kentucky. In 1991 he was moved to Milfer Farm in Unadilla, New York.

Joan and I went to visit The Bid at Milfer Farm in 1998, along with our then fourteen-year-old daughter, Mandy. I wanted to make sure she saw the "greatest horse to ever look through a bridle" at least once in her life. The Bid, then twenty-two and milky white, was led out of his stall and proceeded to nuzzle up against my daughter. He no longer was among the elite roster of stallions as he had been when he was retired to Claiborne Farm with such great promise. And he no longer bore even the slightest resemblance to that charcoal-gray three-year-old with the star on his forehead. But he still held his head high with pride, and when he looked at you, that fire and spirit of his youth still shone through. He was Spectacular Bid, and he still knew it. And you knew it.

Milfer Farm's owner, Dr. Jon Davis, told us at the time, "I still get goose bumps standing next to him." The Bid's devoted groom, Tim Stewart, added, "All you have to do is be around him to know he's something special."

The last image I have of The Bid is him standing outside his barn, his white mane blowing in the breeze, with my daughter standing alongside, patting him on his neck. That moment, like his death in 2003, rekindled memories of a very special time, not only for my wife and me, but also for Thoroughbred racing.

Seattle Slew, Affirmed, and The Bid. They're all gone, and with them the end of a golden era. We will never see the likes of Spectacular Bid again. But at least I have a photo album I can open and show my daughter. And I can tell her, "You remember these pictures of you and this great white horse named Spectacular Bid? Well, his trainer once called him the greatest horse to ever look through a bridle. It was quite an outrageous comment at the time. But, you know what? He was right."

2

A Thorn in Cordero's Rose
(1985)

By 1985 Angel Cordero Jr. had already won two Kentucky Derbys, aboard Cannonade in 1974 and Bold Forbes in 1976. Nine years after his last victory in the Run for the Roses, and after six unplaced finishes in the famed race, he was preparing to ride the brilliant speedball Spend a Buck. The colt was coming off two runaway victories at the newly opened Garden State Park, which had been rebuilt following a fire that destroyed the grandstand.

To promote Garden State Park and attract top horses, track's owner Robert Brennan was offering a $2 million bonus to the owner of any horse that captured the Kentucky Derby and Garden State's three stakes for three-year-olds — the Cherry Hill Mile, Garden State Stakes, and $1 million Jersey Derby, run Memorial Day weekend.

Unlike Cordero's two previous Kentucky Derby winners, who were trained by Hall of Famers Woody Stephens and Laz Barrera, respectively, Spend a Buck was trained by a thirty-three-year-old newcomer named Cam Gambolati, who was just starting up his own stable after having worked in his father's orange groves and for the National Football League's Tampa Bay Buccaneers as a statistician. Spend a Buck's owner, Dennis Diaz, was another newcomer to the sport who had retired at age thirty-eight after a career in insurance, real estate, and citrus farming.

Although Cordero would go on to notch his third Kentucky Derby victory aboard Spend a Buck, who turned in one of the most dominant performances in the race's history, it still remains a conflicting memory for the Hall of Fame rider.

Cordero picked up the mount on Spend a Buck the previous October in the Young America Stakes at the Meadowlands. The colt had begun his career at Calder Race Course, and after three victories in four starts he headed north in search of fame and fortune. Following stops at River Downs and Arlington Park, where he won the Cradle Stakes and Arlington-Washington Futurity, respectively, he suffered a narrow defeat in the Young America Stakes before concluding his two-year-old campaign with a close third in the inaugural running of the Breeders' Cup Juvenile.

Despite those two defeats Cordero saw Spend a Buck's potential and wanted to stick with him. After the Breeders'

Cup he told Gambolati that the colt wasn't changing leads properly. They had him checked and discovered a bone chip in his right knee. On November 26 the chip was removed by arthroscopic surgery, and the colt was sent to Betty and Ralph Sessa's Circle S Farm near Davie, Florida, not far from Calder, to recuperate.

After walking for several days, Spend a Buck was put on a swimming program and soon was back galloping. When he was ready to work, Gambolati called Cordero and asked him if he could come to Florida to work the horse. Although Cordero had just broken his finger, he didn't want to risk losing the mount, so he flew down.

In his first start back, on March 23, Spend a Buck finished third in the seven-furlong Bay Shore Stakes at Aqueduct. Two weeks later he won the Cherry Hill Mile by more than ten lengths. He returned to Garden State two weeks after that, where he romped by 9½ lengths in the Garden State Stakes, blazing the 1⅛ miles in 1:45⅘, the fastest nine-furlong Derby prep ever.

The Kentucky Derby that year drew a deep, talented field, headed by Chief's Crown, as well as top-class colts Proud Truth, Tank's Prospect, Eternal Prince, Skywalker, and Stephan's Odyssey. So strong was this field that two of the starters — Proud Truth and Skywalker — would go on to win Breeders' Cup Classics.

Despite the quality and depth of the Derby field, two-year-old champion Chief's Crown, brilliant winner of the Blue Grass Stakes in near-track-record time, was the overwhelming early favorite. Many felt Spend a Buck and

Eternal Prince, wire-to-wire winner of the Gotham and Wood Memorial, would run each other into submission.

Not having a mount in the Kentucky Oaks, the day before the Derby, Cordero decided to stay in New York to ride and then charter a plane to the Derby. When trainer Jan Nerud, for whom Cordero rode, heard about his plans, he offered to fly him and his wife-to-be, Marjorie, down Friday night on his plane and give them a better deal than they would have gotten with a chartered plane.

Cordero and Margie, who was concluding her brief career as a jockey, packed up following the races and headed for the airport. Shortly after leaving their house on Long Island, Cordero, in his haste to get to the airport, was ticketed for running a stop sign.

"Man, this isn't starting off too good," he said to Margie.

Once they arrived at the airport, Margie took one look at the small five-seat plane and refused to get on. When Cordero told her he wouldn't go without her, she gave in to her fears and reluctantly boarded.

"Look on the bright side," Cordero told her. "If we die, at least we'll die together."

Cordero's agent at the time, Jeff Blum, was new to the business, having been hired only a few months before, and he had booked Cordero to ride a filly in a $100,000 stakes at Garden State Park on the night of the Derby. That meant Cordero, win or lose, would have to catch a plane right after the Derby to make it to New Jersey in time for the race. If he were to win, he would be the first Derby-winning jockey unable to stay for the post-race festivities.

Cordero's main concern in the Derby was getting into a speed duel with Eternal Prince. He knew that Spend a Buck had more natural speed than his foe and could outrun him, but he didn't want the colt to expend too much energy with talented closers like Chief's Crown, Stephan's Odyssey, Proud Truth, and Tank's Prospect in the field. As it turned out, the expected speed duel never materialized. Eternal Prince broke poorly and got swallowed up in the field. That left Spend a Buck and Cordero out there winging by themselves. After sprinting to a big lead while setting blistering fractions, Spend a Buck continued to pour it on, winning by 5¼ lengths. The final time of 2:00⅕ was the third fastest in Derby history.

Before the race Cordero had informed the Churchill Downs stewards he had to leave to fly up to Garden State and wouldn't be able to participate in the post-race interviews, which were held in the press box. They suggested he call the press box and explain his situation, which he did. When the race was over, he jumped off Spend a Buck and raced through the tunnel, where his valet was waiting with his clothes. He caught a taxi and was given a police escort to the airport.

Cordero had arranged with Garden State officials to have a limo driver waiting for him at the airport to drive him and Margie to the track. After landing, they rushed to catch the limo, not realizing Margie had left her purse, containing their money, credit cards, and house keys, on the plane.

Knowing how close he was already cutting it, Cordero began to panic when the limo driver got lost.

"Do you know where you're going?" Cordero asked.

"I'm a little lost," the driver replied.

"You picked the wrong [expletive] time to get lost," said an irate Cordero, who hadn't even had time to shower after the race.

Margie told him to calm down. "Calm down my ass," Cordero said. "The sonofabitch is lost. What kind of driver is he? How can he drive a limo when he don't know where the [expletive] he's going?"

By the time they got to the track, the horses were already leaving the paddock. When Cordero hadn't shown up, Chris Antley was named to replace him on the filly. So, here Cordero had spent thousands of dollars for a plane to get to a race in which he couldn't ride. To make matters worse, Jean Cruguet, after hearing Cordero had a helicopter to take him back to New York, asked if he could catch a ride back. But when Cruguet saw Antley on the filly, he went to the helicopter and told the pilot that Cordero wasn't coming and that he should just fly him back alone.

Not only had Cordero missed the mount, he had no way of getting back home. By then, he was extremely upset and didn't want to talk to the few reporters that were there.

"You have to relax," Margie kept telling him. "You just won the Kentucky Derby and you're all keyed up."

Cordero was then approached by Garden State president Robert Quigley's secretary, who told him, "Look, you've had a long day; why don't you come inside and have something to eat." When Cordero told her he had no way of getting home, she offered to have him flown back to Kennedy Airport on Quigley's helicopter. After eating, Cordero reached in his pocket and gave the waiter $50 of the $60 he had in his wallet.

As they approached the helicopter, Cordero told Margie to give him $20 so he could tip the driver. That's when she realized she had left her purse and wallet on the plane.

After landing in New York, Cordero and Margie decided to go to a nearby hotel that Cordero would often use to put up guests coming from his native Puerto Rico. Not having car keys or house keys, or any money, they used their last $10 to take a taxi to the hotel. Knowing the owner, Cordero was hoping to pay at a later time. But when they arrived, they were told the hotel was booked because of a convention.

Cordero had only one other option and that was to call fellow jockey Jorge Velasquez, who was a close friend. But Velasquez was still in Kentucky, so he called his housekeeper and asked if she had a car. When she told him she did, he asked if she could pick them up and they would stay at Velasquez' house. As it turned out, she got lost, and it took her two hours to find the hotel.

By then, Cordero was livid, as he sat in the hotel lobby, giving Margie dagger looks. Finally, the housekeeper arrived and drove them back to Velasquez' house. When they arrived, it was five in the morning, and Cordero realized he was supposed to work Walter Kelley's good sprinter Ziggy's Boy at six.

Instead of going to bed, he told the housekeeper to give him a ride to Belmont. He arrived at Kelley's barn all disheveled and still wearing his suit jacket.

"Mr. Kelley, I'll be right back. I just have to go to the jockey's room and get some boots," he said to the veteran trainer.

But before he could get another word out, Kelley barked, "You've been out partying all night. Look at you. You think I'm crazy enough to put you on my horse? Go home and go to sleep."

Cordero stopped by Jan Nerud's barn and told his assistant what had happened and that he needed Jan to get Margie's purse to him. But Nerud was off that day, and Cordero was advised not to wake him up. He called Nerud, who was not happy being awakened, and told him it was an emergency; he had no way of getting into his house. Nerud told him where to meet him, but when Cordero came out of the office, he discovered that Velasquez' housekeeper had left. At that point, he needed a ride, so he borrowed Nerud's assistant's car, picked up Margie's purse, and drove to the airport to get his car. He picked up Margie and finally got home, only to run into one final indignity.

As he was about to put the key in the door, it opened, and standing there was his housekeeper. "Don't tell me you've been here," Cordero said to her.

"All night," she replied. "When I saw you win the Derby, I figured you'd need to eat something, so I stayed over and cooked a nice dinner for you, knowing you'd be coming home," She had decorated the house with balloons and signs reading, "Welcome back champ."

Thinking back years later, Cordero said, "I've always hated that Derby. I've been happier after losing the Derby. I loved Spend a Buck, but they didn't even run him in the Preakness. They decided to wait for the Jersey Derby and go for the bonus, and they took me off the horse because I had a commitment to ride Track Barron in the Metropolitan Handicap that day. I asked them to try to hold off and give me a chance to get there for the race, but they decided to put Laffit Pincay on the horse. I lost the mount, a share in the horse, and a share in the bonus, and it cost me nearly ten thousand dollars to fly to Kentucky and back to New Jersey."

But things would change dramatically in Cordero's life to make him think differently about that Derby. In 2001 Margie was tragically killed by a hit-and-run driver near their home in Greenvale, Long Island. Cordero was devastated and still cries for her after seven years. If it weren't for their three children — Julie, Canela, and Angel — and the success of John Velazquez, whom Cordero brought to America, eventually becoming his agent, he doesn't think he would have made it.

Although for some time he had tried to forget the 1985 Kentucky Derby, he now thinks of the race with fond memories, because, as he put it, "Margie was there."

3

······················

The Bald Eagle and the Belmont (1989 and '94)

Charlie Whittingham competed in his first of three Belmont Stakes at age seventy-three, and each time the "Test of the Champion" turned into a test of his patience. Let's just say that the Belmont Stakes is where the Hall of Fame trainer known as the Bald Eagle not only had his wings clipped but also his head ... literally.

Whittingham's first visit to the Belmont was in 1986 with Kentucky Derby winner Ferdinand, who also had finished second to Snow Chief in the Preakness Stakes. The third leg of the Triple Crown looked like an excellent spot for the long-striding, distance-loving colt. But a drenching rain turned the track into a sea of slop, and Ferdinand could do no better than third, beaten 1¼ lengths and a neck by Danzig Connection and John's Treasure, respectively.

When Whittingham returned to the Belmont Stakes

in 1989 with Kentucky Derby and Preakness winner Sunday Silence, he wouldn't have minded an off track one bit, as Sunday Silence had slogged his way through the mud to win the Derby. It was his arch rival Easy Goer whom it appeared the wet going might compromise. The brilliant son of Alydar had finished second in the mud in the Breeders' Cup Juvenile at Churchill Downs and in the Kentucky Derby. So, another off track was the last thing his trainer, Shug McGaughey, wanted.

Leading up to the Belmont, all seemed to be going well for Whittingham and Sunday Silence, other than Whittingham's visits to the first-aid room to treat bites on his leg and finger, compliments of his star performer. His physical encounters with the horse, however, were far from finished. The morning before the race Whittingham was leading Sunday Silence to the track through the tunnel from the paddock. Just as they emerged, Sunday Silence, who was known for rearing on the track and trying to mount his lead ponies, spotted some TV cameramen at the rail, and in a flash, he was up on his hind legs.

As he reared, he nailed Whittingham on the side of the head with his left front hoof, knocking the trainer's cap off. A stunned Whittingham put his hand up to his head, while falling backward, and managed to grab on to the railing. Exercise rider Pam Mabes, unsure what to do, looked back to see if Whittingham was OK. He assured her he was fine and motioned her to keep going.

Back at the barn, Whittingham, more embarrassed than anything else, came out of his office with a smear of iodine on his bald head that complemented the bandage on his finger.

"I zigged when I should have zagged," Whittingham said with a slight grin on his face. "He's done that a lot of times, but I've been a little quicker than him. But today he got me."

Whittingham had been confident Sunday Silence would beat Easy Goer in the Derby, and then after he defeated the Ogden Phipps colt again in the Preakness in one of the great stretch duels of all time, Whittingham made a prediction. "I think we'll win the whole show," he said.

The New York Racing Association used Whittingham's prediction of victory in its ad for the Belmont. More than 1,600 credentials were issued to the media, compared to 1,100 in 1987 when Alysheba attempted to sweep the Triple Crown. The *New York Daily News* had an eight-page pullout on the Belmont, and the *New York Post* also increased its coverage. At the track Sunday Silence and Easy Goer T-shirts were hot items.

By the morning of the race, Whittingham was ready to go home. Not only was he nursing his Sunday Silence wounds, he was losing patience with the crowds constantly gathering around the barn. People actually were walking into the barn wanting to pet Sunday Silence or feed him peppermints.

"I think on the day of the race they should keep everyone out of here," Whittingham said. "All they can do is worry your horse. I'll bet they're not down there bothering Shug's horse."

All week, thunderstorms had rocked the New York area, and steady showers had fallen on Belmont the day before the race. With the track a sea of slop, the chances of a fast track for the Belmont seemed slim at best. That would definitely work in Sunday Silence's favor. But track superintendent Joe King and his crew worked on the track between races Friday and sealed it, packing it down following the last race. They continued to work on it until ten o'clock that night and then returned at four in the morning. The track was closed for training, a decision that wasn't too popular with the trainers. Some speculated all this was being done to dry the track for Easy Goer, who was the house and establishment horse. All morning King's crew harrowed and grated the track, while filling in the areas that had washed out.

By late morning the track had dried out and was listed as fast. Easy Goer loved the surface and Belmont's long, sweeping turns, and all through the race he appeared to be moving over it with more authority than he had at Churchill Downs and Pimlico. Sunday Silence struggled, trying to get past the European import Le Voyageur, and it was obvious this was not going to be a rerun of the Derby and Preakness. Easy Goer sat right behind in third, just waiting for the cue to pounce on his rival. As Sunday Silence stuck his head in front, Pat Day pulled the trigger on Easy Goer, and he flew right past Sunday Silence, opening up a clear lead approaching the quarter pole. It was no contest after that. Easy Goer continued to draw away, winning by eight lengths in 2:26, the second-fastest Belmont of all time.

Easy Goer became the hero Easterners thought he'd be before the Triple Crown. But Whittingham and his "black" colt got their revenge in the Breeders' Cup Classic at Gulfstream Park, nailing down Horse of the Year honors.

When Whittingham returned for another crack at the Belmont Stakes in 1994 with Kentucky Derby runner-up Strodes Creek, he thought he had seen and experienced it all. But Belmont had more surprises and unpleasantness in store for the Bald Eagle.

Strodes Creek, a massive, long-striding ridgling (a horse with one or two undescended testicles), was lightly raced and still immature, but he was a talented horse who seemed to be improving with every start. The son of Halo took up residence in the same barn as Santa Anita Derby winner Brocco, one of the leading contenders for the Belmont.

Arthur Hancock, owner of Sunday Silence, also owned Strodes Creek, in partnership with Rose Hill Stable and Whittingham. Hancock loved to be around the horses and get as up close and personal with them as he could. One morning at Churchill Downs before the Derby, Hancock had been leading Strodes Creek around the shed when the horse stopped for a drink of water. "Get him out of there, Arthur," Whittingham snapped. "He'll drink all the water he can, that hard-headed sonofabitch."

Fortunately for Hancock, he wasn't around the barn the Sunday before the Belmont. Though still six days away, the Belmont had already victimized Whittingham, then eighty-one years old, just as it had in 1989. Two days earlier he had been taken to North Shore Memorial Hospital shortly after watching Strodes Creek work, suffering from a severe stomach ailment. Following a series of tests, he was diagnosed with nothing more than a virus and was released that same morning.

Whittingham, a former Marine, was still as tough as ever. NYRA vice president Terry Meyocks had driven Whittingham's wife to the hospital. When they arrived, Whittingham, despite being in extreme discomfort, had assured Meyocks he'd be back at the barn by feed time. Five hours later he was at the barn as promised.

"He's a tough old son of a gun," the doctor had told Meyocks. "We had six doctors check him out from head and toe and he's fine."

So, here it was two days after his trip to the hospital and Whittingham had just sent Strodes Creek out for a two-mile gallop with exercise rider Sonia Simmons aboard. Whittingham stood on the track in front of an enclosure the trainers called the barbecue pit, perhaps because of all the acerbic gossip that went on in there. I positioned myself right next to him, hoping to get some priceless Whittingham gems for my story.

Then, from the barbecue pit came the words no trainer wants to hear: "Somebody just got off their horse."

Whittingham didn't seem too concerned, not with all the horses on the track. "I hope it's not mine," he said half in jest.

I looked through my binoculars, and, sure enough,

there was Whittingham's exercise rider Sonia Simmons standing on the track with Strodes Creek, one leg held off the ground, in apparent distress. The horse appeared to be hunched over.

"Hey, Steve," trainer Rusty Arnold called from the barbecue pit. "I think that's Charlie's horse."

I told him it was.

"Are you going to tell him?" he asked.

Not having much backbone, I told Rusty I wasn't about to tell Charlie Whittingham his horse had broken down.

Rusty called to Whittingham, "I think that's your horse, Charlie."

Several seconds later the horse ambulance reached the scene. "There's nothing I can do for him over there," Whittingham said, and he turned and headed back to the barn to wait for the ambulance to arrive.

"I don't know what happened," Whittingham said while walking back. "He just went by here galloping as nice as can be. He was as sound a horse as there was on the grounds. This is all we need, right?"

The ambulance arrived at the barn the same time as Whittingham. Sitting on a tack box was a stunned Randy Winick, trainer of Brocco. "What happened?" he asked. But no one had any idea.

The door of the ambulance opened and Strodes Creek was backed out. Oddly enough, he was walking fine, as if nothing had happened. He looked as sound as he had walking to the track. He was led in his stall, where Whittingham checked him out. "Nothing here. He's walking alright on it," he said.

Sonia explained that the horse "just stopped, and his whole body hunched up, with his right leg just hanging there."

What was encouraging to Whittingham was that the horse's leg hadn't become swollen and he was not sweating between the legs as he came off the van. Whittingham had Strodes Creek walk down the shed, and he walked perfectly. So, what happened?

"He might have just stung it," Whittingham said.

Sonia talked to several people, including the veterinarian, and the consensus was that Strodes Creek, being a ridgling, had somehow hit his undescended testicle, which could have accounted for the hunching of the body and holding his leg up in the air.

"It seems very bizarre," she said, "but that's the only conclusion we could come to."

In a touch of irony, Strodes Creek wound up running in the Belmont and finishing a solid third behind Tabasco Cat and Go for Gin while his barn mate, Brocco, was forced to miss the race after suffering a stone bruise the morning before.

So, Whittingham had survived another bizarre occurrence at the Test of the Champion. He would never return. The legendary trainer died of leukemia five years later at age eighty-six. As for Strodes Creek, he will always be remembered as the horse that finished third in the Belmont Stakes six days after being taken off the track in an ambulance.

4

....

Waiting for Arazi
(1992)

My first Kentucky Derby writing assignment for the *Daily Racing Form* was collaborating with my colleague Ed Fountaine on a daily "Derby Patrol" column in 1992, for which we would report on and analyze all Derby works at Churchill Downs.

Although we witnessed the majority of the Derby horses going through their final drills that year, it was all a prelude to the event racing fans and members of the media in America and Europe were anxiously anticipating — the return of undefeated French superstar Arazi, whose electrifying run in the previous fall's Breeders' Cup Juvenile was still being talked about five months later.

Arazi had blown by the entire field, going from thirteenth to first with one of the most explosive bursts of speed ever witnessed in this country. His powerful move brought accolades even from European horsemen.

Trainer John Hammond, who had won the Prix de l'Arc de Triomphe with Suave Dancer, said, "I've never seen anything like it. I have to admit I was a doubter before the race, but this horse must have some incredible engine."

Said Geoffrey Gibbs, senior handicapper for the British Jockey Club, "That was the best two-year-old performance I have seen and am ever likely to see. I have never witnessed such acceleration."

Alex Scott, who had saddled Sheikh Albadou to win the Breeders' Cup Sprint earlier in the day, said, "If we had seen that on our racing soap opera *Trainer*, we'd say it was ridiculous; that sort of thing just doesn't happen. But it did happen. It was like something out of *National Velvet.*"

Not only was my colleague Ed one of many on the Arazi bandwagon, he was standing up and leading the charge. One night after dinner he drove to the makeshift quarantine facility that had been set up for Arazi across the street from Churchill's main gate.

"Just think, that's where Arazi is going to be in a couple of days," he said, sounding as if he were awaiting Elvis.

"You have to stop being so starstruck," I told him.

The fact is I felt Arazi had no chance in the Derby although I wanted him to win as much as anyone else, knowing the history he would make by becoming the first foreign-trained horse to win the Run for the Roses.

Prior to Arazi's Breeders' Cup victory, owner Allen

Paulson had sold half-interest in Arazi to Sheikh Mohammed for a reported $9 million. Shortly afterward the colt underwent knee surgery to remove bone chips, a procedure his trainer Francois Boutin felt was unnecessary.

Prior to Arazi's three-year-old debut, the one-mile Prix Omnium at Saint-Cloud Race Course, Boutin told England's monthly video *Racing World* that Arazi's knees were more problematic after the surgery than before.

Excerpts of his interview were published in the *Racing Post*. "Personally, I don't think Arazi's knees are any better now than they were before," he said. "If anything, they are more of a problem now. Before, he had perfectly good knees, but since the operation, he has been feeling the effects. One minute they are hot and the next minute they are cold."

After his quotes were published, Boutin attempted damage control, stating he had been misinterpreted. But the interviewer, Jocelyn deMoubray, insisted there had been no misinterpretation. He did defend Boutin by saying the trainer had been in a "nervous state" as Arazi's debut grew nearer and pointed out that the interview had been conducted several weeks earlier.

Arazi won the Prix Omnium with ridiculous ease, barely raising a sweat, and would have to go into the Derby off only one prep. The last horse to win the Run for the Roses with less than two starts as a three-year-old was Morvich in 1922. In addition to having little racing foundation, he had never been farther than 1 1/16 miles and was now stretching out to 1¼ miles.

When you added everything up and looked beyond all the hype and glamour that surrounded the horse, there was no way Arazi would go on to win the Derby — unless, of course, he was some kind of freak who could defy all logic and reasoning.

Prior to Arazi's arrival at Churchill Downs, most of the focus was on Santa Anita Derby winner A.P. Indy, trained by Neil Drysdale for Japanese owner Tomonori Tsurumaki, and Casual Lies, the Cinderella horse owned and trained by the unknown and witty Shelley Riley, from the Northern California fair circuit.

Arazi was scheduled to arrive in Louisville on the Sunday afternoon before the Derby. Everyone was well aware that once he had arrived and cleared quarantine, bedlam would rule at his barn and on the racetrack whenever he appeared.

I had arranged with Bob Bailey, head of Churchill Downs security, to shadow him all day and record all the events leading up to and including Arazi's arrival.

On a cold, blustery afternoon, with biting winds that made it feel even colder, Arazi was scheduled to arrive at Butler Field in Louisville at two o'clock. All of Louisville was abuzz waiting for the much-anticipated arrival of the French wonder horse. At 1:30 Bailey looked out his office window toward the old J.J. Carter moving and storage building, which would serve as Arazi's quarantine facility. He called stall superintendent Mike Hargrove to check on Arazi's whereabouts and was informed the plane was on time. Bailey would be responsible for Arazi once the colt arrived at Churchill Downs, and the waiting made him all the more anxious.

Fifteen minutes later Bailey began getting antsy and tried to contact Louisville police officer Boone Pike, who was in charge of coordinating traffic and blocking off nearby Rodman Avenue. There was still no word on Arazi. Bailey, attempting to keep himself occupied, called Lieutenant Don Burbrink and Officer Tom Coin of the Louisville Police Department, who were on special assignment for Churchill Downs. Bailey went over last-minute instructions with them on how the barricades would be set up.

With that taken care of, Bailey called out to his associate Ron Gnagie in the next room. "What are we forgetting, Ron?" he asked. "I'm sure we're forgetting to do something. I've been going over and over everything in my mind."

At 2:40 Bailey learned that the plane had landed but the van hadn't yet left the airport. "Let's get that horse here already," he said to no one in particular. At 3 o'clock the phone rang. Bailey quickly picked it up and said nothing. After hanging up, he called out to the main communications room: "Call dispatch. Tell Boone they're on their way." He then grabbed his coat and headed across the street.

A crowd had begun to form outside the J.J. Carter building. Some seventy chilled-to-the-bone reporters and photographers, many dressed in heavy coats and sweaters, paced back and forth, trying to keep warm. Among them was Ed, equipped with his disposable camera, ready to record the historic moment.

Two uniformed Murray guards from the private security firm hired by Churchill Downs guarded the building's entrance. Soon, the crowd swelled to well over a hundred. People driving down Central Avenue looked quizzically at this unusual gathering. Bailey stood by the curb, peering up the street. He then received word that the van had just exited the Waterson Expressway. At 3:35 Bailey announced what everyone had been waiting hours to hear: "They're here."

Finally, the van was in sight. It stopped outside the quarantine facility, and as the doors slid open, there, staring down at the large crowd, was the one and only Arazi. He quickly was led off the van, as security officers and Churchill employees kept everyone at bay. Just like that it was over. Arazi was tucked away in his new home for the next twenty-four to thirty-six hours. One of the wildest and wackiest Derby weeks had begun.

As hectic as Arazi's arrival had been, it couldn't compare to his first visit to the track. No horse in memory had ever made such an entrance. Hordes of people followed him from the barn to the track. You couldn't get near the rail, which was lined four and five deep.

Wherever Arazi went, the crowds followed, whether he was headed to the track or being bathed outside his barn.

Neil Drysdale remained quietly confident, and it didn't

bother him in the slightest that A.P. Indy was being ignored. Unlike the smallish, compact Arazi, A.P. Indy was a powerfully made colt who looked like he'd run all day.

As I made my way back from the track following Arazi's grand entrance, I passed Drysdale's office and told him he had missed all the excitement. "Oh, I missed it?" he said with a straight face. "I was too busy doing the crossword puzzle."

After a week of Arazi and more Arazi, Derby Day finally arrived. But as soon as I arrived at the backstretch early that morning, the word had already circulated that all was not well with A.P. Indy and that Drysdale would be holding a press conference in the recreation hall to announce the colt had been scratched.

Very few reporters and photographers show up on the backstretch on Derby morning as their work is done until the race. So, only a handful of people were there for Drysdale's announcement. Accompanied by his wife, Inger, and Tsurumaki, Drysdale issued a statement saying A.P. Indy had bruised the inside of his left front hoof and would not run.

Inger tried to hide her tears behind her sunglasses, but the pain became too much to bear. She removed her glasses and wept openly. When Tsurumaki went over and embraced her, she buried her face in his shoulder. A short while later, after returning to the barn, she attempted to express her feelings.

"This business is so … it's cruel," she said. "As blasé

as Neil may seem about the whole thing, you know he's not. In all the years he's been training, this is the first time he's come so close. But I guess it's part of life. I just wish people had really gotten to know him. I guess we'll just have to pick up and go on."

To this day, you'll be hard pressed to find anyone who doesn't believe A.P. Indy would have won the Derby, especially after Casual Lies, whom A.P. Indy had beaten twice in California, finished second, beaten only a length by Lil E. Tee.

As for Arazi, he finished eighth but still provided one of the greatest Derby moments I have ever experienced. Just as he had done in the Breeders' Cup Juvenile, he unleashed a move that had to be seen to be believed. But this time he did it with one sweeping move on the far outside, at least seven or eight paths off the rail. As he went from seventeenth to third in about a quarter of a mile I could actually feel the grandstand shake. But it wasn't shaking as much as my binoculars. We were indeed witnessing the second coming. Pegasus was sprouting wings right before our eyes.

But then Arazi collided head on with reality, and his breathtaking move came to an abrupt halt. The little French colt was mortal after all.

As a postscript to the Derby, A.P. Indy's bruise turned into a quarter crack, from which he recovered and captured the Peter Pan Stakes at Belmont. He was ready to prove to the world in the Belmont Stakes just how special a horse he was.

A week before the race Drysdale scheduled a six-furlong work for A.P. Indy, but a torrential downpour the night before turned the Belmont track into a quagmire. Drysdale had A.P. Indy stabled in the stakes barn, and an early morning check revealed an empty stall, with no sign of the horse. He wasn't at the track and he wasn't in his stall. I located his groom behind the barn and learned that A.P. Indy had been vanned to Aqueduct.

Drysdale had driven to the Big A to check out the condition of the track. Amazingly, it hadn't rained much there, and the track was listed as fast. I drove the fifteen to twenty minutes down the Belt Parkway to Aqueduct, and although I didn't get there in time for the work, I did get there in time to see the priceless smirk on Drysdale's face as he walked off the track with the horse. He knew he had pulled a fast one on everyone. While several of the other Belmont starters had to postpone their works because of the sloppy track at Belmont, A.P. Indy managed to get in a strong six-furlong drill over a fast track at Aqueduct. Two weeks later he captured the Belmont Stakes on his way to Horse of the Year honors.

It would take eight years, but Drysdale finally got his Kentucky Derby win in 2000 with Fusaichi Pegasus. The horse he defeated, Aptitude, was a son of A.P. Indy.

Arazi would go on to win two more stakes in France, but the aura of greatness that surrounded him prior to the Kentucky Derby was gone.

He did return to America later in 1992 for the Breeders'

Cup Mile, where he was sent off as the 3-2 favorite. But he tired to finish eleventh and soon after was retired to Sheikh Mohammed's Dalham Hall Stud in Newmarket, England, where he sired Congaree, one of the most brilliant horses of his era.

5

Bayou Blues
(1993)

I have had the misfortune to be present for arguably the three most tragic breakdowns ever witnessed on American racetracks — Ruffian in the 1975 match race with Foolish Pleasure, Go for Wand in the 1990 Breeders' Cup Distaff, and Barbaro in the 2006 Preakness Stakes. Sadly, another has been forgotten by most racing fans. But for me and many others whose lives he touched, the scars left by Prairie Bayou's fatal breakdown in the 1993 Belmont Stakes remain as deep.

Perhaps it was his gentle nature and the affection people close to the horse had for him. Just spending a short time in his presence, you couldn't help but bond with him.

The most indelible image I have of Prairie Bayou is of him walking off the van on the Wednesday before the Preakness Stakes. His chestnut coat glistened in the late-morning sun, his muscle lines were tightly drawn, and his eyes were wide and bright as he surveyed his new surroundings. A horse could not have come out of the Kentucky Derby in better condition.

Prairie Bayou, the blue-collar gelding who had vaulted to stardom after running all winter over Aqueduct's inner track, was coming off a fast-closing second in the Derby. The son of Little Missouri had gone off as the 4-1 favorite at Churchill Downs after scoring victories in the Jim Beam and Blue Grass stakes.

Here he was at Pimlico to avenge his Derby defeat, in which he had come from sixteenth in the nineteen-horse field to catch longshot Wild Gale for the place spot, behind winner Sea Hero. Prairie Bayou had developed a large fan base, being sent off as the favorite in seven of his previous eight starts going into the Preakness. Despite getting beat 2½ lengths by Sea Hero in the Derby, Prairie Bayou still went off as the 2-1 favorite at Pimlico.

Accompanying the gelding to Baltimore was his groom and friend Roy Brewer, whose nickname for Prairie Bayou was "Dog." Brewer had given him that name because the horse was like a puppy from the day Brewer began taking care of him. And what better sounding name, he thought, than Prairie Dog?

"This horse has such a big heart, it's unbelievable," Brewer said. "It's so nice to be around him because he's so laid back and does whatever you want him to. When he rides in the van, he likes to stick his head out the window. He's got his head out there with his mane blowing in his face and people are waving at him and honking their horns."

At Churchill Downs, Prairie Bayou would come on the track each morning and stand motionless with his head down. Brewer said everyone thought he had gone sour because of the way he was acting. But that was just him

"If he didn't have a saddle towel with his name on it, you'd think he was an outrider's pony," Brewer said. "The only time we ever flew him, some water from an air vent started dripping on his back, and he never even as much as moved his eyes."

Brewer grew up two blocks from Churchill Downs. In the morning and afternoon he could hear the announcements from the backstretch over the loudspeaker. When he was fifteen, he began working on the backstretch during the summer, doing various jobs. The following year he started working regularly, despite everyone at school telling him he was crazy getting up at 4:30 every morning. After graduating high school he decided to work at the track full time, but the salary in Kentucky wasn't very good, so he packed up and headed to New York, where he landed a job with Tom Bohannan, who would become private trainer for John Ed Anthony's powerful Loblolly Stable.

When Brewer returned to Kentucky with Prairie Bayou for the 1993 Derby, it was his first time home in four years. As he came on the track before the race, some two hundred friends and family members in the stands began shouting his name.

Now, he was at Pimlico, once again with the favorite. Brewer took a spot on the rail near the finish line and watched the race on the infield screen. Around the far turn, he saw a horse moving fast on the outside but couldn't tell who it was. The picture on the screen was blurry, and all he could make out was a yellow cap. That was good enough for him. He figured it was either "Dog" or Sea Hero, so he began cheering on the good chance that it was Prairie Bayou.

As they got closer he was pretty sure it was Dog.

"I think that's him," he shouted.

Then he saw the familiar golden chestnut coat and the sweeping stride of Prairie Bayou as he charged up alongside Cherokee Run.

"Yes, it's him," he exclaimed, his flailing arms smacking someone wearing a cowboy hat in the head. Prairie Bayou began edging away from a stubborn Cherokee Run and won by a half-length.

Brewer was about to start running on the racetrack when several people pulled him back. The same thing had happened at Turfway Park after the Jim Beam. When he started to run on to the track, people began screaming at him that the other horses still hadn't crossed the finish line.

After the post-Preakness celebration, a proud Brewer led Prairie Bayou back to the barn area and couldn't believe what he was seeing. The horse was trying to rear and was bouncing along with his neck arched as if he hadn't even run. That evening he cleaned up his dinner in about forty minutes, and the following morning he polished off his breakfast in less than fifteen minutes.

Later that morning Brewer led Prairie Bayou on the van for the five-hour ride back to Belmont Park. As they were about to leave, assistant trainer Todd Graves stepped up on the van and squirted Brewer with a water gun. It would be a fun trip home.

Anthony gave Brewer 1 percent of the winner's share, and the groom proceeded to throw a barbecue for the other grooms, giving them either $20 or a shirt.

"I made about six grand, and I want to spread it around and not let it go to my head," he said.

Back home at Belmont, Prairie Bayou continued to flourish. In his previous ten starts he had seven wins and three seconds, and it would take a lot to beat him in the 1½-mile "Test of the Champion."

One morning Prairie Bayou came out on the track for his final Belmont work with his jockey, Mike Smith, aboard. As the gelding walked along the outside rail, he stopped, turned his head, and looked up at Smith. The horse had unusually tender and expressive eyes. Smith leaned down and affectionately grabbed Prairie Bayou's ear with his right hand, then put his left arm around his neck. This was not a scene you see every day on the racetrack, and the image was captured beautifully by photographer Barbara Livingston.

"He's incredible," Smith said to a couple of bystanders.

"You could put your baby on his back and wouldn't have to worry at all."

Prairie Bayou had this kind of effect on people, and that's what made the tragic events of Belmont day all the harder to accept.

It was a bleak, wet afternoon, and as the field headed down the backstretch in the 125th running of the Belmont Stakes, all anyone could see through the murk was the faint image of a horse being pulled up. No one seemed to know which horse it was or what had happened. Surely, no one could have thought it was Prairie Bayou, one of the soundest, most durable three-year-olds seen in years. This was a horse that enjoyed every second he was on the track and simply loved being a racehorse.

Brewer, after seeing that it was Prairie Bayou, rushed onto the track, but this was under much different circumstances than after the Jim Beam and Preakness. After they put Prairie Bayou in the ambulance, Brewer went up front. He couldn't bear to get in the back with the horse. At first he had no idea how bad it was, but then he heard over the two-way radio what they were going to have to do. He couldn't stand the thought of witnessing it, so he had the driver drop him off near the training track, and he walked back to the barn alone.

Word came a short while later that Prairie Bayou had fractured his left front cannon bone, his long pastern, and both sesamoids. There was nothing anyone could do for him, and a distraught Anthony gave the OK to have him euthanized.

That night, Brewer, still shocked and in tears, stared into Prairie Bayou's empty stall, unable to come to terms with what had happened. Anthony awoke in the middle of the night and sat there wondering whether he had done everything humanely possible to save his horse. Although aware of the hopelessness of the situation, Anthony remained haunted for weeks after the race by the decision not to attempt to save him.

"You never truly realize how close you become to a horse, a dog, or even a friend until they're gone," he said. "Here was a horse who was honest, dependable, and so gentle. When you saw him in the morning, he was always so excited and went to the track with such enthusiasm. I admired him greatly and even loved him. I grieve for Loblolly Stable, and I grieve for racing itself. I didn't realize what a following the horse had and how many people were drawn to him because of his honesty and courage. He was a hard-trying, blue-collar horse who made everyone around him feel good."

Months after the race Smith still became emotional whenever he thought about Prairie Bayou. "Even to this day, I still get choked up when I talk about him," he said. "He was such a great horse to be around, and everyone on the backstretch knew him. I'd come to the barn and watch his gallop boy and groom play with him. They'd take him out in the yard and he'd nudge on them and roll around. He just had a good time with them out there."

Bohannan was so shaken he couldn't even talk about it. His old boss, Rusty Arnold, could sympathize with him.

"I've known Tom for many years, and I know he's taking this really bad," he said. "Everyone feels for him."

But no one grieved for Prairie Bayou more than Brewer. The morning after the race he still was visibly shaken, going about his chores as if in a daze. He walked over and gently stroked the forehead of an unraced Northern Baby two-year-old and then went over and gave his filly, Aztec Hill, a pat on the neck.

"Whew! I didn't expect that," he said, taking a deep breath. He then looked at the hand-painted sign hanging outside Prairie Bayou's empty stall that read: "Prairie Bayou: 1993 Preakness Winner."

"I've got to get rid of that sign," he said. "It hurts just to look at it. I couldn't even eat last night."

Prairie Bayou's death has all but faded from memory, as have many of his accomplishments. But he is a horse worth remembering for all he gave of himself and the impact he had on the Triple Crown trail.

He is buried at Dr. Gary Lavin's Longfield Farm in Goshen, Kentucky, where he was born and raised.

6

Derby Doings Dither
(1994)

I still vividly remember that afternoon in the late winter of 1993 when *Daily Racing Form* editor George Bernet, who happened to be a close friend, called me into his office.

"I just got off the phone with Joe Hirsch," he said. "Joe's exact words were, 'I'm unable to do "Derby Doings" any longer; give it to Steve.' "

It is difficult to explain just how big a deal this was to me. Joe is a legend in the sport, probably the most legendary turf writer of all time. He had started "Derby Doings" nearly forty years earlier, and for him finally to relinquish it due to poor health and hand it over to me was the ultimate honor.

"Derby Doings" was a spring fixture in the *Daily Racing Form,* and its format had never been duplicated by any other publication. For some two weeks leading up to the Kentucky Derby, Joe would write daily reports on all the news pertaining to the Derby hopefuls, with quotes from the trainers. I decided to alter the format a bit, and instead of writing a daily report, I personalized it, injecting it with humor, or at least attempted humor, and human-interest stories.

When I arrived in Louisville two weeks before the 1994 Derby, I pretty much had the coverage of the race all to myself, with the exception of Jennie Rees of the Louisville *Courier-Journal*. Needless to say, I had Joe's enormous shoes to fill, but I felt comfortable heading up the *Racing Form*'s Derby coverage, and I put everything I had into making it not only informative but also entertaining.

Arriving on the Churchill Downs backstretch before dawn, I usually parked alongside Barn 40, where noted Kentucky veterinarian Alex Harthill stabled the horses he owned. Harthill was almost as recognizable at the Downs as the Twin Spires. On one morning I got out of my car and from out of the darkness I could hear someone calling my name. It was Doc Harthill, who was grazing one of his horses a short distance away.

Harthill, who had been the vet for more Derby winners than anyone else in the history of the race, was taking care of the brilliant Irgun, impressive winner of the Gotham Stakes and Wood Memorial.

Irgun was trained by Steve Young and owned by Brandon Chase, who had produced the popular cult film *Alligator*. Chase had named his colt after the Zionist freedom fighters that the British and Palestinians, and even many Jews, considered more of a terrorist organization. The Irgun made international headlines in 1946 when it blew up the King David Hotel in Jerusalem, killing nearly a hundred people, mostly British.

Young had thought it was just a catchy name, pronounced ER-gun. But when Chase told him it was actually er-GOON and was a Jewish terrorist group, it made Young uneasy, especially considering the 1993 World Trade Center bombing by radical Islamic terrorists that had occurred the previous year. Young couldn't help but think what might happen if the story behind the name got out and the horse won the Derby. "I don't want anyone taking a shot at me in the winner's circle," he said.

His concern had turned to fear when New York Racing Association security received a death threat against the horse prior to the Wood Memorial.

Irgun had come out of his Wood Memorial victory with a foot abscess. Before sending the colt to Kentucky, Young asked New York Racing Association veterinarian William O. Reed if he could recommend a vet to use at Churchill Downs. Reed recommended Harthill, with whom he had been friends since college.

The foot bruise became public knowledge, but from all early reports Harthill seemed to have it under control. However, there was more to the story, as I would find out on this particular morning.

"Hey, Steve," Harthill called out. "You gotta help me.

Normally, I would have told Joe this, but maybe you can do something. You gotta make them scratch this horse. I work for the owner, and I can't do anything; my hands are tied. Not only does this horse have that foot bruise, he's got a fever, too."

"How can I make them scratch the horse?" I asked. "What am I supposed to do?" I'm sure Joe would have known what to say and what to do, but I definitely was in over my head; more so than I thought.

I later found out that Young and Harthill had been at odds. According to Young, Harthill actually was in favor of running the horse, but Young wouldn't go along with the veterinarian's methods to get the colt to the race. Young considered Irgun his "buddy" and was trying to protect him as well as keep jockey Jerry Bailey from riding an injured mount, even though the trainer stood to lose $400,000 on a future book bet he had made before the colt even started. In addition, he insisted the horse never had a fever or was sick in any way and that Harthill, unable to "treat" the colt the way he wanted, was now trying to get him scratched.

I was just trying to cover my first Derby as lead writer, and here was the trainer of one of the favorites and his veterinarian telling completely different stories. I always got along well with Harthill, but I also saw the affection Young had for Irgun and was convinced he would never do anything to jeopardize the colt's safety. Heck, he was willing to take a bullet for the horse.

As it turned out, it all became moot when Irgun came

down with another abscess on the same foot and was scratched.

Another of the many scenes that played out in that year's wild Derby was Jerry Bailey's choice of mounts. Bailey had been the regular rider of Go for Gin, piloting the colt to easy victories in the Remsen Stakes at two and the Preview Stakes at Gulfstream in his three-year-old debut. But that was followed by a second in the Fountain of Youth Stakes and a fourth in the Florida Derby.

Following the Florida Derby, Bailey landed the mount on Irgun in the Gotham Stakes. He thought nothing of it, as the colt had had only two career starts and was coming off a second-place finish in an allowance race at Santa Anita. But in the Gotham, Irgun, a magnificent-looking chestnut son of 1983 Kentucky Derby winner Sunny's Halo, destroyed his opposition, winning by six lengths. Just like that, Bailey had himself another Derby horse. He told Young how impressed he was with Irgun, but he was committed to ride Go for Gin against him in the Wood Memorial. He would decide on whom to ride in the Derby after that race.

For the Wood, Young used Gary Stevens, knowing he was committed to ride Santa Anita Derby winner Brocco at Churchill Downs. Young was confident that Irgun would convince Bailey to switch mounts. For the entire 1⅛-mile distance of the Wood, Bailey chased Irgun but was unable to catch him, losing by 1½ lengths. It didn't take long after the race for him to jump ship and sign on to ride Irgun in the Derby. Go for Gin's trainer, Nick Zito, who had won the Derby three years earlier with Strike the Gold, immediately went shopping for another rider and decided on Chris McCarron, who had ridden Alysheba to victory in the 1987 Run for the Roses.

As we all know, Irgun never made it to the Derby while Go for Gin, taking advantage of a sloppy track, sloshed his way to a two-length victory, leading almost every step of the way. The Derby gods no doubt were smiling down on Go for Gin and Zito, as the other classy speed horses in the race — Holy Bull, Smilin Singin Sam, and Valiant Nature — all ran into trouble at one point or another and were unable to get anywhere near the lead, allowing McCarron and Go for Gin to cruise around there by themselves.

The controversies surrounding that year's Derby weren't over. To this day Jimmy Croll, trainer of Holy Bull, insists that someone got to his horse, which accounted for the lethargic way he acted before and during the race. Holy Bull, of course, went undefeated the rest of the year on his way to a spectacular Horse of the Year campaign.

It was also a Derby that had three titans from the entertainment field — songwriter Burt Bacharach, who owned Soul of the Matter; Motown Records founder Berry Gordy, owner of Powis Castle; and Albert Broccoli, co-producer of the James Bond films, who owned Brocco.

Also in the field was the roguish Tabasco Cat, who had

run over trainer D. Wayne Lukas' son, Jeff, one morning at Santa Anita, putting him in a coma for two weeks and nearly killing him. Lukas, who had been mired in the worst slump of his career, going 2½ years without a grade I victory, gathered his crew together and told them not to take it out on the horse. He worked long and hard with the colt, and although Tabasco Cat could finish no better than sixth in the Derby, he went on to win the Preakness and Belmont. Ironically, the horse that ended Lukas' slump was the one that almost killed his son. Lukas would go on to win a remarkable six consecutive Triple Crown races from 1994 to 1996.

So, that was my first Kentucky Derby as lead writer for the *Racing Form*. You can't say I didn't have anything to write about.

7

Blinkers
(1995)

In 1995 the Preakness barn was pretty much devoid of horses until the Wednesday before the race when Kentucky Derby stars Thunder Gulch and Timber Country arrived from Louisville. By that time, a six-year-old black Labrador named Blinkers had taken over the stakes barn.

One hundred and twenty pounds of joy and jowls, Blinkers made his presence felt immediately. Owned by Derby runner-up Tejano Run's trainer, Kenny McPeek, and his wife-to-be, Sue, he would spend each morning making his rounds of the barn — cavorting, begging, and gorging himself on doughnuts, muffins, bagels, and any other handout he could find. He even managed to muscle his way into an interview on WBAL, a Baltimore radio station.

Blinkers became such a media hound that word began to spread outside the track about McPeek's pushy pooch, and before long, Blinkers' lovable puss was plastered all over the local TV stations and newspapers. The Blinkers phenomenon took off from there. By Preakness day he had become a national celebrity with write-ups in the *Wall Street Journal*, *USA Today*, and the *Los Angeles Times*. He even received a large bouquet of flowers and a card from two yellow Labradors from Tuxedo, New York.

The nearby Cross Keys Inn, where McPeek and Sue were staying, didn't allow dogs, so the couple had to sneak Blinkers in and out every day. One day a hotel employee heard Sue call out, "Come on, Blinkers." As she approached, Sue thought they had been caught. Instead, the employee said excitedly, "Hey, isn't that the dog with Tejano Run?"

One morning McPeek showed up at the barn without Blinkers. Everyone wanted to know where the dog was, and the trainer had to answer more questions about Blinkers' absence than he did about his Kentucky Derby runner-up. The morning before, Blinkers had wolfed down four bran muffins, washing them down with a drink from Preakness starter Mystery Storm's water bucket. McPeek reported that Blinkers likely had one bran muffin too many and had come down with a case of what I dubbed the "Tejano runs."

When the two D. Wayne Lukas horses — Kentucky Derby winner Thunder Gulch and third-place finisher Timber Country — arrived at Pimlico, the focus of the media attention turned to the two colts. But Blinkers was not about to give up the spotlight easily.

One afternoon Lukas took Thunder Gulch out to graze at the same time Blinkers was playing "fetch" with a tennis ball. Just as Thunder Gulch headed through the opening in the fence and onto the grass, Blinkers went chasing after the ball and darted right in front of him, causing the Derby winner to rear several times. Needless to say, Lukas was neither pleased nor amused.

Timber Country went on to win the Preakness, with Thunder Gulch finishing third. Tejano Run was never in the race and finished ninth. It didn't take long for Blinkers to get over his buddy's defeat. After the race Lukas popped the corks on several bottles of champagne while his then wife, Shari, cut into a victory cake presented to them by Pimlico. The lure of food and beverage quickly made Blinkers forget his loyalties and wander pitifully into the enemy camp at the other end of the stakes barn looking for a handout.

Shari had just cut a slice of cake, placed a napkin under it, and was looking for someone to give it to. When Blinkers came running over, she reached down and gave him the slice. Blinkers, wide-eyed and panting with excitement, wolfed down the cake ... and the napkin, then returned to join his entourage.

Having married a short time later, McPeek and Sue lived in a small house with a fenced-in yard, right alongside the entrance to the Waterson Expressway in Louisville, just a few minutes from Churchill Downs. I often drove by the house after leaving the track and would look to see if Blinkers was in the yard.

On March 30, 2003, the McPeeks had to put Blinkers to sleep. The infirmities of old age had slowed him to the point he could function no longer.

Even after fifteen years, I think of Blinkers whenever I'm on the Pimlico backstretch covering the Preakness, especially when members of the media come walking out of the hospitality room with doughnuts or muffins in hand.

Returning to Pimlico every spring, I can't help but feel the presence of those who have come before, whether it's a trainer, a horse, or even a dog. I've been fortunate to come in contact with many great horses at the Preakness over the years, going back to Secretariat and Spectacular Bid. But I'll remember Blinkers as much, if not more, than any of them.

8

Song and a Prayer
(1996)

The draw for the 1996 Kentucky Derby had just concluded, and as if he hadn't had enough misfortune since arriving at Churchill Downs, Unbridled's Song drew the outside post in the twenty-horse field. This was the final indignity for a horse who had been the star three-year-old all winter and the solid Derby favorite.

Bob Baffert, trainer of Santa Anita Derby winner Cavonnier, shared a barn with Unbridled's Song and was witness to all the colt's travails. Following the draw, Baffert had seen enough. Fun-loving and quick-witted, he seemed perplexed as he walked out of the room at the Sports Spectrum, where the draw was held, and asked, "How can any horse in my barn have such bad karma?"

That pretty much said it all. Baffert, a relatively unknown trainer at the time, had become smitten with Unbridled's Song after the colt's impressive victories in the Florida

Derby, the Wood Memorial, and the previous year's Breeders' Cup Juvenile. Although Baffert had confidence in his California-bred gelding, Unbridled's Song was in a different stratosphere. After watching the handsome gray work six furlongs one morning, Baffert stated emphatically what he'd do to get a horse like this: "I'd swim across a river of gasoline with a torch up my ass."

It was Baffert who first noticed more than a week before the Derby that Unbridled's Song was wearing a bar shoe — a special shoe that further protects the hoof. Up to that point, everything had seemed to be going smoothly for the son of Unbridled, who was owned by the brazen and outspoken newcomer Ernie Paragallo and trained by the soft-spoken Jim Ryerson, who was making his second appearance in the Derby, having saddled Meadow Flight to an eleventh-place finish in 1994. Paragallo was tall, dark, and brooding and always dressed in black. He spoke with a thick New York accent and rarely smiled, but I found him to be a breath of fresh air. An investment banker and computer software executive, he stormed onto the racing scene, buying expensive yearlings at the sales and quickly gaining a reputation as a rebel who dared to defy the establishment. No one knew whether to take him seriously when he guaranteed that Unbridled's Song would not only win the Derby but also sweep the Triple Crown.

I had gotten to know Buzz Chace, Paragallo's bloodstock agent, adviser, and stable manager, pretty well in 1994. Chace had picked out Meadow Flight (for Leonard

Pivnick) and Unbridled's Song as yearlings and spent a good deal of time with both colts after their arrivals at Churchill Downs.

Chace had helped get Unbridled's Song settled at Churchill Downs until Ryerson arrived and immediately requested the colt be stabled away from all the hoopla of the Derby barns. The colt had been placed in the barn of April Mayberry, who also played host to Baffert and Cavonnier.

Each morning Unbridled's Song went out to train at 5:45 under the cover of darkness. No one thought much of it until Baffert shared his observation about the bar shoe. It was eight days until the Derby, and, although Unbridled's Song seemed fine from what little anyone could see, the bar shoe had to be addressed.

Ryerson was in the office when I showed up at the barn, so I waited. I saw Chace standing several yards away and asked him: "So, Buzz, I hear Unbridled's Song is wearing a bar shoe."

"Bar shoe?" he responded with a quizzical look. "I don't know anything about a bar shoe."

Well, we knew he was wearing one. Jennie Rees of the Louisville *Courier-Journal*, whose husband trained at Churchill Downs, had also been made aware of it. There are no secrets at the Derby. So, the only thing to do was to wait for Ryerson to come out of his office. When he did, several reporters gathered around for what was to be a standard interview. Jennie and I looked at each other, trying to figure out who was going to blurt out the bar-shoe question. Finally, I casually asked, "How long has he been wearing a bar shoe?"

Ryerson always seemed to have a smirk, and it grew wider as he realized the word was out. He proceeded to explain that Unbridled's Song had injured his foot in the Wood Memorial. Ryerson said he thought he must have hit something on the track and taken out a chunk of the bulb of his heel.

His groom, Jose Perales, had discovered it while picking the colt's feet out after the Wood. Unbridled's Song was given a tetanus shot and an acrylic patch to help his foot heal. Because there was some warmth in the foot, they had to drain it. Fortunately, there was no fever and, therefore, no need to administer antibiotics. When the colt had worked two days earlier at Churchill Downs without the bar shoe, the foot was "cold as ice" afterward.

That's the way I understood the situation as I prepared for dinner with Ryerson and Chace at Pat's Steak House the Monday before the Derby. My *Daily Racing Form* colleague, Ed Fountaine, and I had decided to invite Chace and Ryerson for dinner on a night of their choosing. Ed was a huge fan of Unbridled's Song and was doing a diary with Ryerson for the *Form*, and he thought this was a good way to show the paper's appreciation.

Ryerson and Chace showed up about an hour late. To say this dinner was brutal would be a gross understatement. You could have cut the tension with one of Pat's steak knives. Chace, smoking one cigarette after another, stared out the window the entire night without saying a word. Ryerson, not known for his verbosity, engaged in minimal conversation, and the perpetual smirk and far-off look on his face told us this was the last place he wanted to be.

Ed and I were so uncomfortable we kept alternating trips to the men's room. The flushing of the toilet turned out to be the most stimulating sound we heard all night. My primary objective was to pick at my salmon and accompanying veggies and make them last. As long as I had food in my mouth, the endless silence didn't seem quite as awkward. Ed did the same with his steak. Chace went through so many cigarettes and stared out the window for such a prolonged period that the smoke bounced off the window and hovered over my dinner, giving "smoked salmon" a whole new meaning. When the ordeal, mercifully, was over, Ed and I just shook our heads. "What the hell was that all about?" I asked.

All we could think of was that maybe Unbridled's Song's foot had taken a turn for the worse that afternoon. As it turned out, it had. When Ryerson returned to the barn that afternoon and checked the horse's foot, he noticed tenderness in the area, so he pulled off the shoe and soaked the foot. He put the colt on antibiotics, something no trainer wants to do that close to a race, especially the Derby. The blacksmith, Hans Albrecht, feeling the old shoe was aggravating the heel, replaced it with a Z-bar shoe, which, with its Z-shaped extension inside the shoe, provides even more protection. It wasn't looking good for the Derby favorite.

The following morning (Tuesday), the foot seemed better and Unbridled's Song had a good gallop with his new shoe. At first he was a little tentative with it but appeared to get used to it quickly. Ryerson did say that the colt would not breeze Wednesday as originally planned, which was not good news. If he had to miss the breeze altogether, they would be forced to come up with an alternate plan.

Meanwhile, another scene was being played out on the opposite end of Barn 33. Baffert had flown to Phoenix a week before the Derby to saddle a horse in a stakes and was contacted by bloodstock agents J.B. and Kevin McKathan, who were at the Ocala two-year-old sale. They wanted to let him know about a Silver Buck colt they loved and to ask if he was interested in bidding on him. Baffert had been burned buying horses sight unseen and had vowed never to do it again. The McKathans sent a videotape of the colt working for the sale to Baffert's hotel in Louisville, but by the time he was able to watch it, the sale was over.

Chace had flown down to the sale with Paragallo, and he, too, liked the colt. He met with the consignors and asked how much they thought he would bring. They said they thought he was worth $75,000 to $80,000. When the colt came into the ring, Chace bid on him for Paragallo, but the price soared above $90,000. Chace turned to Paragallo and said, "Ernie, the guy is bidding us up. They don't have any live bid on the horse."

Turned off, they both agreed to forget it and stopped

bidding. As a result, the $100,000 reserve placed on the colt wasn't met. When Baffert returned to Louisville and watched the video, he fell in love with the colt and figured he had blown it until J.B. McKathan told him the colt had been bought back.

Still, Baffert was unsure of the breeding and wanted reassurance. When he saw Chace, he asked his thoughts on Silver Buck as a sire. Chace told him he really didn't like him but added that any horse can get a runner.

Baffert had the McKathans offer $80,000 for the colt, and the deal was done. Now he had to find someone to sell him to. Baffert, knowing Chace had liked the colt enough to bid on him, asked whether he was interested in buying him for Paragallo or one of his other clients.

Chace told him he would ask Paragallo if he wanted the colt. If he did, he'd be paying pretty much what he originally had intended to pay. Paragallo was due to arrive in Louisville the following morning, and Chace told Baffert he was pretty sure he'd take him.

Later that day Baffert arrived at the barn only to discover that Unbridled's Song had suffered a setback. The following morning, as the colt's foot was being soaked, Baffert went over to Chace and told him he was sorry they were having such a tough time with the horse but he was wondering whether he'd spoken to Paragallo about the two-year-old. Chace wasn't feeling any more sociable than he was at our dinner the night before and told Baffert to find another buyer. He said it wasn't a good time and he didn't even want to bring it up to Paragallo.

So, Baffert wound up selling the colt, already named Silver Charm, to Robert Lewis.

On Tuesday night Ryerson called Paragallo and told him he was thinking of changing plans and working Unbridled's Song a half-mile early Wednesday morning. Sure, he could have played it safe and galloped him over the track, which was on the wet side from an early morning shower. But Ryerson thought it was time to find out once and for all just where they were with the colt. This was the Kentucky Derby. If Unbridled's Song's foot wasn't able to stand up to the punishment of a half-mile work, he had no business being in the race. Paragallo gave him the go ahead, and when Ryerson awoke Wednesday morning he contacted jockey Mike Smith to come work the horse.

It was still dark, with a light rain falling on Churchill Downs, when Smith showed up at the barn. It created a foreboding atmosphere knowing that a horse with a nagging foot bruise, and wearing bar shoes, was about to work over a wet track. Unbridled's Song was under tack by six. The Z-bar shoe had been replaced with two egg-bar shoes the night before by the blacksmith. Egg-bar shoes are full egg-shaped shoes that cover the entire foot and provide better balance and support. Some horsemen think they do not hinder a horse's performance, while others equate the transition to going from running shoes to combat boots.

Ryerson had been up most of the night worrying about the work. He went up to the clocker's stand and waited.

"We'll know in a few minutes," he said. Time wasn't important. He just wanted to see how the colt went with the egg-bars and how the foot stood up to the pressure.

In the clocker's stand were trainers Phil Thomas and Gary "Red Dog" Hartlage, who had their clocks ready to time Unbridled's Song. All anyone could see of the work were the split seconds when the colt passed under the lights situated at the poles. Unbridled's Song broke off at the half-mile pole. It was near impossible to catch the opening-quarter split from their vantage point in the dark, so they timed his final three-eighths. As Thomas and Hartlage checked the splits, they couldn't believe what they saw and were convinced they had blown the time or had picked up the wrong horse.

"No, that's him," Ryerson assured them. As Unbridled's Song passed the finish line, Thomas looked at his watch first and said, "Good God! I got his last three-eighths in :33⅘."

"I got the same thing," Hartlage said with amazement. Ryerson checked with the clockers, who told him they had caught the colt in :46 flat for the half-mile, galloping out five furlongs in :59⅕. It was a spectacular work for any horse, but for one wearing two egg-bar shoes and nursing a sore foot it was unheard of. One independent clocker caught him pulling up six furlongs in 1:11 and change, with Smith finally able to rein him in after a mile in 1:37 and change.

Everyone was buzzing over the time of the work and the way he galloped out, but Ryerson remained apprehensive.

The most important part was still to come. "The time means nothing," he said. "It's all how he comes back."

Then, out of the fading darkness, a gray figure appeared, bouncing along next to his lead pony Leo. "He looks all right ... he looks all right!" Ryerson said, his voice rising with renewed enthusiasm. When Smith gave him a big thumbs up leaving the track, it put the finishing touches on what turned out to be one heck of a morning.

Unbridled's Song cooled out beautifully, and veterinarian Foster Northrop said the colt came out of the work in excellent shape. Ryerson had used the two egg-bar shoes because they were what Unbridled's Song would wear in the Derby, and he needed to know what kind of effect they would have on him.

Unbridled's Song made it to the Derby, and although he finished fifth as the 7-2 favorite, he ran an amazing race, pressing an extremely fast pace and opening up a clear lead on the far turn. But it was obvious as soon as he changed leads after turning for home that his stride was shortening. The pace, breaking from post nineteen (following a scratch), and the cumbersome egg-bar shoes had combined to do him in. In spite of everything he had gone through, he was beaten less than four lengths and only a neck and a nose for third.

Baffert nearly pulled it off with Cavonnier, who, despite getting lashed across the face with another rider's whip, was beaten a nose on the wire by the D. Wayne Lukas-trained Grindstone. Baffert, as everyone knows, returned the following year and won the Derby with the colt he had tried to sell to Paragallo.

For Jim Ryerson, the 2006 Kentucky Derby was a stressful affair that left him emotionally drained. Churchill Downs had set up a podium outside his barn, where the trainer would address the media on the latest condition of his horse. Now, it finally was over. All that remained from the previous week's soap opera was the familiar podium that had become a meeting place each morning for every reporter, photographer, and TV cameraman on the backstretch. Curled up inside the podium, fast asleep, was Ryerson's black cat, Lucky, whose conflicting color and name served as the final reminder of one of the strangest weeks in the history of the Kentucky Derby.

9

......

Louie, Nicky, and the Streak (1996)

Wayne Lukas was on a roll unlike any other in the history of the Triple Crown. After breaking out of a 2½-year drought during which he did not win a single grade I stakes, Lukas captured the 1994 Preakness Stakes with Tabasco Cat. That victory started an amazing winning streak of six consecutive Triple Crown races, including the Belmont Stakes with Tabasco Cat. The following year Thunder Gulch won the Kentucky Derby, Timber Country took the Preakness, and Thunder Gulch won the Belmont Stakes. Lukas extended his streak in 1996 when Grindstone captured the Kentucky Derby.

The last trainer to win a Triple Crown race prior to Lukas' streak was his archrival, Nick Zito, who won the 1994 Kentucky Derby with Go for Gin. Now, Zito was looking to end the streak in the Preakness Stakes with Louis Quatorze. Despite the colt's poor effort in the

Derby, in which he finished sixteenth of nineteen starters, Zito was willing to throw out the race. The Derby often produces uncharacteristically sub-par performances, and Zito was hoping Louis Quatorze would return to his earlier form, which saw him finish second to Skip Away in the Blue Grass Stakes at odds of 8-1.

Although Grindstone came out of the Derby with a career-ending chip in his right knee, Zito knew Lukas would still be well armed for the Preakness with Prince of Thieves, third in the Kentucky Derby; Editor's Note, sixth in the Derby; and Victory Speech, tenth in the Derby but third in the Fountain of Youth and Jim Beam stakes.

Zito, who had won the Derby with Strike the Gold and Go for Gin, did not want to take any chances going into the Preakness. He had Louis Quatorze's blood tested and showed off the results, pointing out the excellent hemoglobin count. With nothing in the horse's blood that could have caused the dull performance, it was on to the second leg of the Triple Crown.

A new Preakness trend had been started in 1992 and '93 when trainer Tom Bohannan shipped Pine Bluff and Prairie Bayou, respectively, to Pimlico the Wednesday before the race. Prior to that, most horses shipped to Baltimore a day or two after the Derby. When both horses won the Preakness, other trainers began following the same schedule. In 1995 Lukas shipped Timber Country and Thunder Gulch to Pimlico on the Wednesday before the Preakness, and that, too, proved successful, resulting in a one-three finish, respectively.

In 1996 Zito prepared for the Preakness in the old-fashioned manner by sending his horse to Baltimore early to train over the track. Zito was running Star Standard in the Pimlico Special the Saturday before the Preakness, so he shipped him, Louis Quatorze, and Saratoga Dandy to Pimlico several days before the Special.

Louis Quatorze was owned by William Condren and Joseph Cornacchia in partnership with the colt's breeder, Georgia Hofmann. Condren and Cornacchia also owned Star Standard and Saratoga Dandy, as well as Go for Gin, and were partners in Strike the Gold with B. Giles Brophy.

It was odd seeing only three horses stabled in the stakes barn, which housed the vast majority of the Preakness starters each year, along with most of the other horses shipping to Pimlico for stakes. Although Zito had toyed with the idea of running Saratoga Dandy in the Preakness as well, the trainer opted to go for the 1 1/16-mile Sir Barton Stakes on the same card.

Shortly after arriving in Baltimore, Zito began thinking of a rider to replace Chris Antley, who had ridden Louis Quatorze in the Derby. While debating whether to use Mike Smith or Alex Solis, Zito heard that Lukas had informed Pat Day's agent, Doc Danner, he was taking Day off Prince of Thieves and replacing him with Jerry Bailey, who had masterfully ridden Grindstone at Churchill Downs. Grindstone's retirement had left Bailey available. Although Day had ridden Prince of Thieves well in the Derby, Lukas said he thought his chances of extending his Triple Crown winning streak would be better with the hot Bailey. Day was bitterly disappointed but publicly stated he understood Lukas' decision.

"Wayne wants to keep his streak alive and feels this was his best opportunity," said Day, a born-again Christian who always thanked a higher source for all his successes. "He told me it was a coaching move, and I can't blame him for that."

But inside, Day was not happy, feeling he had a big chance to win with Prince of Thieves, on whom he had done nothing wrong in the Derby.

On the Saturday before the Preakness, Day rode Star Standard to victory in the Pimlico Special for Zito. The following morning Danner left a message for Zito informing him of Lukas' decision and Day's availability if the trainer wanted him. Zito called Danner back and said "definitely."

On Tuesday, Zito sent Louis Quatorze out for a five-furlong work with exercise rider Jamie Sanders aboard. Louie turned in a super work — five furlongs in :59⅘, galloping out a strong six furlongs in 1:13⅕.

"I love him," Zito said, watching from the grandstand. "I can't believe this horse. He has so much ability; he's got to run big. If he doesn't, I'll be extremely disappointed. I also like the fact that he's not nervous here. With no other horses in the barn, he feels like he's at his own private training center."

As Louie walked back along the rail, Zito said to

Sanders, "That was the best I've ever seen him work."

"He was tough," Sanders replied. "You saw how strong he galloped out, and I was pulling him up after the wire. If I had let him go in the stretch, he would have gone in :57 and change. "

With Grindstone and the Kentucky Derby favorite Unbridled's Song out of the Preakness, the big names were Cavonnier, who had been beaten a nose in the Derby, Prince of Thieves, and Skip Away, despite his twelfth-place finish in the Derby.

Cavonnier arrived from Kentucky on Wednesday, with Lukas' trio shipping in on Thursday. It was apparent that Louis Quatorze and Skip Away were the speed of the race. If one were able to get a clear lead, he'd have a big advantage. If they hooked up, they could very well cook each other, setting the race up for closers such as Cavonnier, Editor's Note, and Prince of Thieves. At the post-position draw, Zito was thrilled when Louis Quatorze drew post six, with Skip Away stuck on the outside in post eleven. Skip Away's trainer, Sonny Hine, who had raced at Pimlico for years, knew he was in trouble.

"I just hate the outside at Pimlico, with those sharp turns, but what can you do?" he said. "God willing, he'll get a good trip, but what's to be will be."

Preakness day arrived, and Zito, having already won the Pimlico Special and having the post position draw go in his favor, was feeling good about his chances. His confidence continued to grow when Saratoga Dandy won the Sir Barton Stakes earlier on the card, making it two for two for Zito with his three early arrivals.

Before the Preakness, Zito told Day, "If you can get the lead, excellent. If you're second, that would be good. If you're third, that would be fair."

Zito later would say Day "went for excellent."

Day gunned Louis Quatorze out of the gate and charged to the lead. Sonny Hine's worst fears came true when Skip Away was bumped repeatedly by Prince of Thieves and never could get position going into the clubhouse turn. The speedy gray had to settle in second while an unchallenged Louis Quatorze set testing fractions of :46⅕ and 1:09⅘. It was a two-horse race all the way. Skip Away challenged nearing the top of the stretch, pulling on near-even terms, but Louis Quatorze had plenty left. He opened up again and drew off to a 3¼-length victory, equaling the fastest Preakness ever run.

As Louie drew clear in the stretch, Zito, watching from the porch outside the jockey's room, began throwing a flurry of punches into the air, shouting, "Ride with the angels, Pat ... ride with the angels. You're gonna get there."

It was as if a surge of electricity had hit Pimlico. Zito, one of the most popular trainers in the country, if not the most popular, rushed to the track, kissing and high-fiving everyone. With his fists clenched, he kept pointing to the heavens. Zito was every working stiff's best friend; the kid from the streets of New York who made good with nothing but his own sweat and tireless dedication.

As Zito made his way to the winner's circle, Lukas came over and put his arm around his longtime rival and said, "If my streak had to be broken, I'm glad it was you who broke it."

Ironically, it was Zito who had won the last Triple Crown race (with Go for Gin) before Lukas started his streak, and it was Zito who ended it. And it was Day who began Lukas' streak, winning the Preakness aboard Tabasco Cat, and it was Day who ended it.

10

Silver and Gold
(1997)

During the three weeks between the 1997 Preakness and Belmont stakes, all eyes were focused on Silver Charm, as the powerful gray prepared to try to become racing's twelfth Triple Crown winner. What most people failed to realize, however, was that this year's Triple Crown was destined to be a tale of two horses.

Behind the scenes, a hard-nosed bay colt named Touch Gold was on a collision course with Silver Charm's quest for immortality. With his foot held together by glue and wire, Touch Gold would test not only the Kentucky Derby and Preakness winner but also my loyalties.

Touch Gold had begun dropping hints of promise in Keeneland's Lexington Stakes. Gary Stevens, who was looking forward to riding Silver Charm in the Derby, guided Touch Gold to an explosive 8½-length victory, blowing right by eventual sprint champion Smoke

Glacken after six furlongs in the 1¹⁄₁₆-mile race. So powerful was Touch Gold's performance that Stevens, not relishing the thought of facing the colt at Churchill Downs, suggested to trainer Dave Hofmans that he was not quite ready to go 1¼ miles in the Derby thirteen days later, which most likely was correct.

The Lexington was only Touch Gold's second start of the year; his first was a six-furlong allowance race at Santa Anita, which he had won by four lengths in 1:09⁴⁄₅.

Touch Gold did skip the Derby to prepare for the Preakness while Silver Charm scored a gutsy neck victory over the favored Captain Bodgit in the Run for the Roses.

Now it was time for Touch Gold to get his crack at Silver Charm in the second leg of the Triple Crown. With Chris McCarron aboard, Touch Gold took one step out of the gate and stumbled so badly his nose actually hit the ground, sending up a spray of dirt. What happened after that proved Touch Gold was no ordinary horse. After dropping back to last in the ten-horse field, he made a bold move and charged up to the leaders down the backstretch, only to lose his momentum after finding himself in tight quarters.

Rounding the far turn, Touch Gold shifted into another gear and moved into contention along the rail. Shortly after turning for home, Kent Desormeaux, on Free House, looked back over his left shoulder. Seeing Touch Gold moving up behind him, he closed the hole.

Touch Gold had to check sharply, brushing against the rail, but, remarkably, the colt still had another run in him. He matched strides with Free House, Silver Charm, and Captain Bodgit in the final eighth, and although he couldn't gain on them, he was beaten only 1½ lengths for all the money, in what remains the greatest losing effort, along with Seattle Slew's Jockey Club Gold Cup, I have ever seen.

Touch Gold's stumble and remarkable performance were overshadowed by the heart-pounding finish that saw Silver Charm thrust his head in front right at the wire to defeat Free House and Captain Bodgit, putting himself in position to become racing's first Triple Crown winner since Affirmed in 1978.

What made Touch Gold's performance all the more impressive was he came out of the race with an ugly quarter crack, the result of hitting the back of his front foot with his hind foot when he stumbled at the break.

The Preakness incident and subsequent injury hit me hard. Though I'm supposed to be objective when covering races, it was tough when it came to Touch Gold.

Two years earlier I had come up with the idea to write a two-part feature for the *Daily Racing Form* centering around one yearling from the 1995 Keeneland July yearling sale catalog. I would fly to Kentucky three or four weeks before the sale, meet with his consignor, and visit the colt at the farm. After learning everything I could about him — such as his pedigree, physical attributes and deficiencies, and temperament — I would write the first part of the feature. Then, returning to Kentucky for the sale, I would follow his progress, observing him being shown to prospective buyers and learning more about him by talking to his handlers. The story would conclude with his sale.

After scrutinizing the entire catalog for a colt that would not be a sale topper but had an interesting pedigree, I chose a colt by Deputy Minister out of the Buckpasser mare Passing Mood, who was being pinhooked by agent John Moynihan after the colt's purchase as a weanling for $180,000 at the previous year's Keeneland November breeding stock sale. That colt would later be named Touch Gold.

Moynihan, who was part owner of Walmac Bloodstock Services, had bought the colt in partnership with Hill 'n' Dale Sales Agency. He drove me out to Bedford Farm near Paris, Kentucky, where the colt was being prepared for the sale.

Having been a weanling purchase, he was placed in a private paddock so as not to get bullied by the other young horses that had been raised together. Moynihan had bought the colt, born in late May, despite his smallish size. He had grown steadily since the purchase and looked impressive when they brought him out to show me.

I returned home and wrote my story, providing as many details and observations as I could, and then returned for the sale several weeks later. The weather was brutally hot, and most buyers took every opportunity to cool off in the clubhouse dining room or in the pavilion.

At 10:30 a.m. the day before the colt was scheduled to sell, Frank Stronach, along with his manager, Mike Doyle, showed up to look at him. The colt, who had always been aggressive and a bit ornery, spent most of his time outside pulling hard on the lip chain and twisting his head. Cherise Gasper, head of sales for Walmac, explained to Stronach and Doyle that the yearling habitually tried to bite his handler.

"He's a nice kind of horse, though," Doyle said nonchalantly. It was obvious he and Stronach liked what they saw. The following day, as the colt was being readied for his big moment, he still was trying to bite his handler, Greg Partain. "He can really get on your nerves," Partain said as he put the finishing touches on the colt.

While the colt was being walked outside the pavilion, Stronach and Doyle came by for one last look and received some final words of encouragement from Gasper. With Moynihan watching outside the pavilion, Stronach bought the colt for $375,000.

"Letting him grow is probably the most important thing right now," Doyle said.

And grow he did, from a solid stakes-placed two-year-old in Canada to a grade II winner in the United States to one of the contenders for the Preakness and Belmont stakes.

So, here he was, the colt I had picked out of a sale catalog and followed, now one of the top three-year-olds in the country. This would be as close as I would ever come to the feeling of what it's like to be a bloodstock agent.

With so much history between us, I admit being biased toward the colt as he headed to the Belmont Stakes and his confrontation with Silver Charm. The two-week stretch following the Preakness was not easy for Touch Gold. His quarter crack, which would plague him the rest of the year, was the worst that quarter-crack specialist Ian McKinlay had ever seen. The colt had ripped off a good 2½ inches of his hoof, exposing raw flesh. McKinlay was called in immediately after the Preakness to work his magic. The laminae had been exposed, and the blacksmith had to toughen up the tissue so an artificial acrylic wall could be put on. This required ten days of downtime to allow the hoof to start healing. McKinlay then stabilized the quarter crack so the colt could train on it. Once the hoof got tough enough, he would wire it all together right before the race.

For two weeks McKinlay kept saying how amazed he was by Touch Gold's pugnacity. "He is a tough horse, boy," he said. "It's not the patch that's going to get him to the Belmont; it's his toughness. This horse is a monster. He's so smart that when he wants to get away from you he'll just drop down to his knees. He knows every trick in the book. You have to keep him busy with carrots and things because as soon as he knows you're messing with him, he'll be up to his old tricks."

Eight days before the Belmont Stakes, Hofmans, who took over the training of Touch Gold as a three-year-old from Stronach's Canadian trainer Danny Vella, flew in from California on the red-eye to watch the colt work seven furlongs. The track still was a bit wet underneath following light rain earlier in the week.

When veterinarian Steve Carr showed up that morning to give Touch Gold his Lasix shot, he was in for a battle that would last several minutes. Just hooking the webbing back up after he was finished and escaping unscathed required some fancy and several carrots brought by assistant trainer Darla Elliott, who stuffed them in the colt's mouth during Carr's getaway. Hofmans went up to the box area to watch the work. This would be the first time Touch Gold would be putting pressure on the hoof, and Hofmans just wanted to see how it would stand up.

He was looking for "a nice, slow seven furlongs in about 1:28." He said he'd even be happy with 1:30.

"Work him from the three-quarters past the wire to the mile and three-eighths pole," he told former jockey George Martens, who had won the Belmont in 1981 aboard Summing. "What I want you to do is just sit on him. He'll start taking you around the turn, and you can let him finish from the eighth pole. You can let him gallop out, but he's not a big gallop-out horse."

As Touch Gold galloped into the first turn, with Elliott alongside on the pony, Hofmans told me, "I want him to get a little tired."

Touch Gold broke off running and went his opening eighth in :12⅖. "He's got to be careful," Hofmans said of Martens. "This horse likes to get going around the turn."

Martens kept him well off the rail to slow him down a bit, but Touch Gold rattled off his three-eighths in :35⅘ and half in :48. With Martens not asking anything of him, the colt threw in a quarter in :23⅕, flying past the eighth pole in 1:11⅖ for the six furlongs.

"Geez, that's a lot faster than I wanted," Hofmans said.

Touch Gold kept pouring it on, completing his seven furlongs in 1:23⅘. Hofmans was stunned. "I guess it was a good work," he said. "Let's talk to Georgie and see what he has to say. So much for 1:28."

Martens was surprised by the time because the colt was going so easily. When Elliott heard the time, all she said was, "No!"

Back at the barn, although Touch Gold's bandages were shredded from the wet, sandy track, the patch held firmly and he was walking perfectly sound. But it still was bothersome to the colt, so Hofmans had him take it easy for several days to give the foot time to heal further and allow McKinlay to get it in the best shape possible for the race.

Five days before the Belmont, I decided to fly down to Louisville, along with David Grening of the New York *Post*, to watch Silver Charm's work on Tuesday and then fly back to New York with the colt, who would be the lone occupant on the Tex Sutton-chartered Boeing 727. Mel Prince, who had worked for Sutton for thirty-four years, said flying one horse is extremely rare but this one horse was special.

By 6:30 Tuesday morning, cars were already filing into Churchill Downs at a steady clip. By eight, some 2,500 fans had gathered on the apron and in the grandstand. They were there for only one reason: to see Silver Charm work before his departure the following day for Belmont Park, where he would attempt to become racing's first Triple Crown winner in nineteen years.

Several days earlier Baffert had lightheartedly invited the public to come watch Silver Charm work, unaware that every local TV and radio station would relay that invitation and that the public would flock to the Downs in droves, much to the dismay of track officials. Silver Charm and Baffert had become heroes to Kentuckians, who embraced them with a fervor unlike anything seen before in the Bluegrass State. The charismatic Baffert was mobbed wherever he went, autographing everything from buttons, posters, and photographs to napkins and matchbook covers. One night, a large party at the Executive Inn West Hotel came to a halt for thirty minutes when Baffert was spotted and invited in. People dropped everything and gathered around to get his autograph and wish him good luck.

Baffert's folly in extending an invitation to the public almost cost him dearly. As Silver Charm galloped by the stands, the crowd on the apron let out a loud cheer that spooked a five-year-old gelding named Firecrest, who was walking in the opposite direction along the rail.

Firecrest suddenly bolted and veered right into Silver Charm's path.

Jockey Joe Steiner, aboard the big gray colt, averted disaster by grabbing a hold of Silver Charm and swerving away from the out-of-control Firecrest. The two horses grazed each other, but Silver Charm calmly shrugged it off and went about his business, working five furlongs in a solid 1:01.

The morning after the work Baffert bid farewell to Camelot to embark on the final leg of the journey. He was not looking forward to facing the cold reality of New York and the grueling 1½-mile Belmont Stakes. He just wanted it to be over.

"I feel like the weight of Kentucky is on my shoulders," he said as he entered the gates of the Churchill Downs backstretch at six in the morning. "I wish I could look into the future through a crystal ball. I want it to be two weeks from now, and I want to drive by Esposito's [the popular tavern across the street from the Belmont backstretch] and see what colors they've got hanging up there. Then I can come back to Kentucky, hopefully wearing the Triple Crown on my head."

Baffert arrived at trainer April Mayberry's barn, where he had nine horses stabled, and unloaded his luggage from his Lincoln Town Car. "I feel like I'm going to camp," he said.

After arriving at the airport, Baffert said one final goodbye to Mayberry, who had been taking care of his horses stabled there while he was in California.

"Well, April, this is the end of the road," he said.

On the plane the lone figure of Silver Charm stood out among the dozens of empty stalls. I had flown with horses once before, accompanying Kentucky Derby winner Thunder Gulch, Preakness winner Timber Country, and the star filly Serena's Song — all trained by D. Wayne Lukas — from Louisville to New York.

Silver Charm was relaxed, picking at his hayrack under the watchful eye of groom Rudy Silva, who sat on a chair holding the shank.

"Look at Rudy," Baffert said. "Is he dedicated or what? He hasn't left that horse's side for two months."

Because of his allergies Baffert spent most of the time up front, sitting on a cooler reading a newspaper or talking to Prince and his longtime friend and main client, Mike Pegram.

The plane touched down in New York at 8:50, and as the doors opened, Baffert, unable to pass up a chance at levity, held both arms up, hunched his shoulders, and gave several photographers a Richard Nixon victory sign. Silver Charm was then loaded on the van and given a police escort to Belmont Park, where he was greeted by one of the largest throngs of reporters, photographers, and TV cameramen ever assembled.

All Baffert wanted to do was bed the horse down, check into his hotel, turn off the phone, and go to sleep. But that would have to wait as the media immediately engulfed him upon his arrival. Kentucky was now just a memory. He was in New York, and there was a Triple

Crown to be won.

The Belmont Stakes had been in decline in recent years, with crowds ranging from 38,000 to 40,000. It was Silver Charm who would awaken the "Test of the Champion," attracting a crowd of more than 70,000 and paving the way for the record 100,000-plus crowds that would follow.

Those paying attention to the earlier races on the card had to have an inclination just how good a horse Touch Gold was when Smoke Glacken, whom Touch Gold had destroyed in the Lexington Stakes, won the seven-furlong Riva Ridge Stakes in a blistering 1:20⅘.

Touch Gold had made it through his final week with no mishaps and went to the post with his hoof patched and laced with wire to hold it together. When it was time for him to head to the track, he was stretched out in his stall fast asleep, and Elliott had to rouse him. But by the time he got on the track, he was a bear. He gave McCarron such a tough time, the rider's "right arm went numb" trying to hold him back from the outrider's horse. "He was trying to eat that pony up," McCarron later said.

Before the race Baffert responded to the cheering crowd by tossing Silver Charm buttons down from his box, as the fans below scrambled to retrieve them.

The stage was set. Silver Charm, attempting to sweep the Triple Crown, had to take on his old nemesis Free House once again and also Touch Gold, who many felt was the best horse in the Preakness. The only one missing was Kentucky Derby runner-up Captain Bodgit, who had suffered a career-ending tendon injury after his close third-place finish in the Preakness.

McCarron, breaking from the rail, surprised everyone by going right to the front with Touch Gold, who led around the first turn and into the backstretch. As they continued down the backstretch, Wild Rush, also owned by Stronach but trained by Dick Mandella, went up after Touch Gold, as Stevens let out a notch on Silver Charm who also moved up to challenge, with Free House right on his tail.

Just like that, all three blew right on by Touch Gold, who was now back in fourth, some three lengths off the lead. Around the far turn, Stevens went for it all and moved Silver Charm right up alongside Wild Rush, with Free House still breathing down his neck.

"I got Free House right outside me; the race is on," Stevens yelled over to Jerry Bailey on a retreating Wild Rush.

Meanwhile, McCarron, who had remained in close contact with the leaders along the inside, swung Touch Gold to the outside. Silver Charm began to ease away from Free House as the crowd went wild. Only a furlong to go and Silver Charm looked to be home free. Nothing stood between him and immortality; or so one thought.

Stevens could sense something bearing down on him from the far outside, but he was blocked by a stubborn Free House and couldn't see who it was. He naturally assumed it was the late-closing Louisiana Derby and Arkansas Derby winner Crypto Star. Stevens bore down on Silver Charm, and just as he finally cleared Free House, he looked to his right and was shocked to see Frank Stronach's powder blue silks sweep by him thirty yards from the wire. He couldn't believe it was Touch Gold, who appeared to have called it a day down the backstretch.

Mandella described the final furlong best when he said Touch Gold looked like "a wild dog chasing down Silver Charm and Free House."

As I made my way to the winner's circle, it took awhile for it all to sink in. Like most everyone else, I had wanted to see Silver Charm win the Triple Crown, and that part of me was disappointed. But then it hit me: This was my little yearling. Hiding my elation was difficult, but with so many dejected people all around, I had no choice.

I had relayed my story to Hofmans back at the Preakness, and after the Belmont, much to my embarrassment, he would introduce me to people as the person who picked out Touch Gold. He even introduced me that way to Stronach.

The following morning Touch Gold went out to graze and was fed mints by several visitors. Hofmans showed up and immediately looked at the foot and was pleased to feel no heat in it.

But then McKinlay arrived and sanded and filed down the hoof. He removed the patch with a drill, and what he found convinced him this was the toughest horse he'd ever seen.

"What we healed up, he's basically peeled right off,"

McKinlay said. "It's raw under there now. It looks like a piece of prime rib. The tissue that we got tough enough that it could hold the glue, he jarred and busted it loose. I'll tell you, this is one tough horse; believe me. He's got heart. If you look at him he's walking sound on it. He's an amazing horse."

Silver Charm would not race again until December 26 in the seven-furlong Malibu Stakes, finishing second. The colt was a bad bleeder because of pneumonia he had had as a youngster, and Baffert felt he needed time to let his lungs heal after several bleeding episodes. He would race the following two years, winning a number of major stakes, including the Dubai World Cup. In 2007, he was inducted into racing's Hall of Fame.

McKinlay kept Touch Gold's quarter crack under control, periodically going to California to treat him. The colt returned east in early August to win the Haskell Invitational Handicap, but everything went downhill after that. As McKinlay said, "After the Haskell we were just chasing our tail."

Touch Gold was forced to miss the Travers, and then, at the Meadowlands in the Pegasus Handicap, running on a wet, abrasive track that had to sting him, he aggravated the foot again and just ran around the track to finish last of four starters.

It was decided to keep him in training and point for the Breeders' Cup Classic, which turned out to be a disastrous move. Touch Gold barely picked his feet up during the race and finished ninth. When he returned, he had torn a good portion of his hoof off. It was tough, as well as sad, for me to look at.

The following year, with his foot finally healed, he was turned over to Pat Byrne to train but was suffering from a neurological disorder and never again was the same horse he had been in the spring and summer of his three-year-old campaign. Even McKinlay to this day wonders how great a horse he might have been had he not stumbled in the Preakness.

So ended one of the most memorable Triple Crowns in history, and my lone excursion into the world of "bloodstock agent." I have had many favorite horses since entering the sport in 1967, but I will never be linked to one the way I was to Touch Gold.

11

Lukas' Good Luck Charm
(1999)

As the 1990s drew to a close, three trainers — Nick Zito, D. Wayne Lukas, and Bob Baffert — dominated the Kentucky Derby. Zito won in 1991 and 1994. Lukas scored back-to-back victories in 1995 and 1996, and Baffert did likewise in 1997 and 1998. The trio, collectively, captured six of the decade's last eight runnings.

In 1999, the Derby's 125th anniversary, the three trainers accounted for seven horses in the nineteen-horse field, with the Baffert entry of General Challenge and Excellent Meeting favored at 9-2. The Zito-trained Stephen Got Even was the second choice at 5-1, followed by Baffert's Prime Timber at 6-1 and Lukas' Cat Thief at 7-1. Zito's Wood Memorial winner, Adonis, was 18-1.

One of the longest prices in the field at 31-1 was the Lukas-trained Charismatic, owned by Robert and Beverly Lewis, who two years earlier had captured the

1997 Kentucky Derby with the Baffert-trained Silver Charm. Despite having won the Lexington Stakes in his previous start, Charismatic was lightly regarded, having competed twice for a $62,500 claiming tag. No former claimer had won the Derby since Dust Commander in 1970.

Lukas, uncharacteristically, had put Charismatic in a claiming race at Hollywood Park in the colt's sixth career start and dodged a bullet when the colt romped by five lengths and no one put in a claim for him.

Two and a half months later Lukas tempted fate once again by dropping Charismatic in a claiming race for $62,500 following a dismal effort in the Santa Catalina Stakes. One Santa Anita trainer with his eye on the colt was Mike Mitchell, who was notorious for his numerous raids on the claim box. Mitchell was a bloodhound when it came to sniffing out good claims, and he was all ready to snatch up Charismatic, but something transpired several days before that made him change his mind.

Mitchell was a race car buff, and Lewis, a major distributor for Budweiser, had given him four free tickets to a National Hot Rod Association drag race that had a participant sponsored by Budweiser. Mitchell was so grateful for the tickets he said no way could he claim a horse from Lewis.

But that wasn't the only odd occurrence that prevented Lukas and Lewis from losing the horse that day. Thoroughbred owner Will Wolford, based in Las Vegas and constantly looking for potential claiming bargains, had been following Charismatic. When Wolford saw the colt show up in another claiming race, he called his Kentucky-based trainer, Paul McGee, and told him he wanted to claim the horse and that he should get someone in California to put in the claim for him.

As it turned out, however, Wolford's California owner's license had not yet been processed because the person in charge was on vacation at the time. When Wolford called to inquire about the status of his license, he learned no one had yet gotten to his application and he was not eligible to claim the horse.

Two months after nearly losing the horse Lukas saddled Charismatic in Keeneland's Lexington Stakes, in which he was 12-1 following a well-beaten fourth in the Santa Anita Derby.

The Lewises had all but given up hope of making it back to the Derby. Their big horse, Straight Man, had just eliminated himself from the Derby picture by running poorly in the Gallery Furniture.com Stakes (now the Lane's End Stakes) at Turfway Park. The same weekend Silver Charm was soundly defeated in the Dubai World Cup after bleeding badly in the race. All they had going for them was their former claimer, Charismatic, who, although a rank outsider for the Derby, was beginning to show signs of improvement.

At approximately 1:40 p.m. California time on April 18, Bob Lewis was at home in Newport Beach, waiting for the telecast of the Lexington Stakes later that afternoon. But Lewis had forgotten about the time difference and was surprised to receive a phone call from an excited Lukas.

"What did you think of that?" Lukas exclaimed.

"Think of what?" Lewis responded.

"His performance," said Lukas. "You just won. Watch the race later and call me. It's gonna blow your mind."

Lukas had been trying to convince Laffit Pincay Jr. to ride Charismatic in an effort to get the aging Hall of Famer back to the Kentucky Derby. But Pincay had several mounts lined up at Hollywood Park on the day of the Lexington and had decided to stay home.

"Don't worry about the Lexington," Lukas had told him. "I can get Jerry Bailey to ride him, and he's committed to Worldly Manner for the Derby. There's no sense flying all the way here. We'll just put Jerry on him and go from there."

The day before the Lexington, Lukas had read that Pincay had accepted the mount on Event of the Year in the Mervyn LeRoy Handicap, run the same day as the Derby. He then contacted Chris Antley, who had battled a cocaine problem since the mid-eighties. In 1997, six years after winning the Kentucky Derby on Strike the Gold, Antley quit riding due to a weight problem. After swelling to 147 pounds, he began taking water pills, but they turned his body into a sponge, as he put it, all but sucking the life out of him. After an exhausting exercise program, he was able to get down to riding weight and was beginning to return to his former glory.

Lukas had urged Antley to tune into the Lexington Stakes. "Watch this horse tomorrow," Lukas told him.

"You'll like what you see. I don't want you to come just to ride a horse, but I think he's got a legitimate shot to win the Derby."

Lukas had seen Charismatic's rapid physical and mental improvement in the past month, and he believed the colt had as much of a shot in the Derby, if not more, than his more heralded colt, Cat Thief, owned by William T. Young's Overbrook Farm.

When Charismatic came storming down the stretch to win the Lexington going away, Antley had himself a Derby mount.

At Churchill Downs, I would head for the backstretch every afternoon at 3:30 and go straight to Lukas' barn, knowing he'd be out grazing Charismatic. Lukas has never been known for restraining his enthusiasm when assessing his horses' chances in a race. But this time I could sense his sincerity as he expounded on Charismatic's many virtues.

On a typical afternoon Charismatic would graze contentedly, searching out dandelions and ripping them out by the root. His coat, illuminated by the afternoon sun, was resplendent, and he was obviously flourishing and peaking at the right time.

"Would you believe this horse just ran a week ago and almost broke the track record?" Lukas asked, as he rubbed his hand against the colt's neck and down to his shoulder. "Look at him — there are no stress lines at all. I had to gallop him a mile and seven-eighths today and let him pick it up the last part of it. He carries his weight like

Secretariat. I guarantee you, if he were to win this thing, and I know he's probably nobody's pick, watch out in the next two, because he's one of those horses who will come back in the Preakness with a vengeance."

That would not be the only prophetic comment Lukas would make regarding Charismatic. A few days later, Ronnie Ebanks, the irrepressible agent for jockey Shane Sellers, stopped by, and in typical fashion began to push Lukas' buttons. Ebanks had Sellers on the Florida Derby and Fountain of Youth winner Vicar and was figuring out a way to get Lukas' goat.

He knew Lukas had been talking up Charismatic and decided to make him put his money where his mouth was. He kept knocking Charismatic, and Lukas kept counter attacking. By the time they were through, Ebanks and Lukas had a $2,000 wager, Vicar against Charismatic, horse for horse.

But Ebanks wasn't about to let up. The next morning, he stopped by Lukas' barn to remind him of the stupid bet he had made.

"I'm sure you came to your senses this morning and realize you're in a financially bad situation," Ebanks said to Lukas.

"No, no," Lukas replied. "I don't catch a soft touch like you every day."

Ebanks loved going toe to toe with Lukas. "I led you right into my trap," he said. "I got you fired up, and I know if I get you fired up, that's the best time to get you in a bad bet. Let's get it straight. We got a two thousand dollar bet, horse for horse, whoever finishes in front of the other, Vicar against ... how do you say your horse's name?"

"Don't worry," Lukas shot back. "It'll be a household word by Saturday night."

The Wednesday before the Derby, Lukas' training chores had just ended when Louisville veterinarian Kurt Oliver and his twelve-year-old daughter, Libby, paid him a visit.

"Libby thinks Wayne hung the moon and swung the stars," said Oliver.

As soon as they arrived, Libby went searching the grassy area behind Lukas' barn for a four-leaf clover to give to him for the Derby. It took her less than a minute to return. In her hand was a four-leaf clover. She presented it to a stunned Lukas and simply said: "Good luck."

Amazed at the find, Lukas thanked her and tucked it neatly in his wallet.

Just before bringing Charismatic and Cat Thief to the paddock on Derby Day, Lukas received a visit from Overbrook Farm yearling manager Bruce Jenson, his wife, Nancy, and their nine-year-old daughter, Kenzie.

Kenzie had been battling leukemia for four years, and in 1995 had undergone a bone-marrow transplant, spending two months in the hospital. Since then, she had made steady progress. Before leaving for the track, Kenzie asked Lukas if he had anything she could take with her to hold during the race for good luck.

Lukas remembered the four-leaf clover Libby had given him. He took it from his wallet, wrapped it in paper, stapling the ends, and handed it to Kenzie.

To what degree that four-leaf clover helped Lukas and Charismatic win the Derby is up to each person to decide. Following the race, Kenzie returned to the barn, still clutching her good-luck charm. Kurt Oliver also was there to offer his congratulations. He went over to Kenzie, kneeled down, and said, "You hang on to that and kiss it every night. Libby is twelve, but she's the luckiest person I've ever seen in my life."

Lukas then autographed the paper containing the four-leaf clover and presented Kenzie with a rose from the victory blanket.

An emotional Nancy Jenson couldn't believe the chain of events she had witnessed. "Imagine, one little girl picks up a four-leaf clover and passes it on, and another little girl carries it over to the track," Nancy said. "For Wayne to go out and win the Derby and finish third [with Cat Thief] is very special. I'm just so glad Kenzie was here to see this."

And what about Ronnie Ebanks and his wager with Lukas? As the big crowd began to file out of Churchill Downs, Ebanks, in a quiet corner of the backstretch, was getting into his car. He shrugged his shoulders and said, "All I can do is pay him and say, 'hail to the king.' He got me again."

As for the king himself, he went into his office after the race and called Kunz' restaurant in downtown Louisville. Owner John Kunz had told Lukas if he won he'd set up a room for him and "bring out king crab and champagne on ice — the works."

But Lukas, who had just been elected to the Hall of Fame the week before, decided to celebrate the way he knew best. He canceled the room, returned to his hotel, ordered a burger and chocolate milk, and went to bed.

12

Mike and the Captain
(2000)

The night of the 1997 Kentucky Derby, Mike Pegram attended a victory dinner at John E's restaurant in Louisville with about twenty-five friends and relatives of his longtime friend Bob Baffert, trainer of Derby winner Silver Charm.

Accompanying Pegram was a rather bosomy blonde wearing what could be conservatively called a tight black dress.

Pegram was one of Baffert's earliest clients and the one who had convinced him to venture into Thoroughbreds after numerous successful years as a Quarter-Horse trainer. When Baffert won the Derby for owners Robert and Beverly Lewis, Pegram was as excited for his friend as if he had won the race himself. No one was more jubilant in the winner's circle than Pegram. The year before, when Grindstone beat Baffert's Cavonnier by a nose right on the wire in the Run for the Roses, Pegram, watching on TV, had been so upset he threw his beer against the wall.

The morning after Silver Charm's victory, Baffert held court outside his barn, answering the media's usual questions. A short while later the Lewises showed up with their daughter, Nancy, and her one-year-old daughter, Chloe, to see Silver Charm before flying back to California.

By ten o'clock, everyone had cleared out and Baffert finally was able to take a deep breath and savor his victory. He then went to the gift shop and purchased several Derby T-shirts at the half-price sale.

Pegram had been scheduled to fly home that morning, and Baffert assumed he was on his way. As Baffert stood outside his barn soaking up the sun, his phone rang. Seconds after answering, his face went blank as he listened. "What?" he asked with a tone of disbelief. He was obviously upset about something. He walked away and continued his conversation in private.

On the other end of the call was Pegram telling Baffert he was in jail at the Louisville airport.

"That damn, goofy broad," Pegram told Baffert. "Remember I told you she gave me a gift? Well, I never opened it, and it turned out to be a goddamn gun, so they locked me up."

At the previous night's dinner Pegram's date had given him a present, telling him to open it before he left. But Pegram had either forgotten or decided to wait until he got home. He put it in his flight bag and thought nothing of it. That was until he passed through airport security and was asked to step to the side. The package was opened, and there, neatly packed, was a .357-caliber Magnum.

Not only did Pegram have a gun in his possession but he also was carrying a large wad of bills in his pocket, having cashed in on Silver Charm.

Pegram told Baffert the woman was trying to get him a lawyer, but Baffert said he'd contact Brereton Jones, a former Kentucky governor who was one of the country's top Thoroughbred breeders and owners. Baffert called Jones, who, although about to leave for church, said he'd try to make some calls.

While Baffert was on the phone, Julien "Buck" Wheat, director of horsemen's relations at Churchill Downs, drove up in his golf cart. The ubiquitous Buckwheat was a fixture on the Churchill Downs backstretch and the go-to person for anything. Baffert told him what had happened.

"Don't worry; I'll take care of it," he said. "I got a buddy on the police force."

Buck called his friend Captain Steve Thompson of the Louisville Police Department, who immediately went to the airport and convinced airport security there was no criminal intent, explaining the circumstances.

Pegram was more embarrassed than anything else. Thompson told him as they left the airport and headed to Baffert's barn, "I hope you don't have any bad feelings

Trainer Bud Delp (above) called Spectacular Bid (left, after his Preakness victory) "the greatest horse to ever look through a bridle."

The author snapped the top photo during Preakness week. It shows champion filly Davona Dale pinning her ears at The Bid.

For a long time Angel Cordero Jr. didn't like to think about his winning Derby ride aboard Spend a Buck in 1985. But since the death of his wife (left, center) in 2001, Cordero remembers that race fondly because "Margie was there."

Often called the "Test of the Champion," the Belmont Stakes tested the patience of trainer Charlie Whittingham twice: when the Triple Crown bid of Sunday Silence (above) was on the line and when Strodes Creek (top) was injured and nearly scratched.

All eyes — and cameras — were on Arazi when the French champion arrived for the 1992 Kentucky Derby (left and top). The colt finished eighth.

Ill-fated Prairie Bayou, winner of the 1993 Preakness, captured the author's heart with his gentle nature.

Irgun (top) caused a brief stir in 1994, the year the author began his Derby column.

Unbridled's Song (above) and his foot were the story in 1995.

Trainer Nick Zito (right, with the author,) ended rival D. Wayne Lukas' run of Triple Crown victories with Louis Quatorze (above center) in the 1996 Preakness.

The author had "picked" Touch Gold (left) to follow as a yearling at Keeneland. He felt mixed emotions when "his" horse ended the Triple Crown bid of Silver Charm (below).

Owner Mike Pegram showed his gratitude to Louisville police commander Steve Thompson (above left) by naming a horse Captain Steve. Pegram and trainer Bob Baffert (left) shared Derby glory in 1998 with Real Quiet.

Charismatic won the 1999 Derby for Bob and Beverly Lewis and trainer D. Wayne Lukas (below).

The 2000 Kentucky Derby was bittersweet for exercise rider Andy Durnin (above, with trainer Neil Drysdale), who quieted the rambunctious Fusaichi Pegasus during Derby week. Fusaichi Pegasus won, but a few weeks later Durnin lost his mentor, Eddie Gregson (above, inset).

To ensure Monarchos had every chance of winning the 2001 Kentucky Derby, trainer John Ward (above) assembled a team (right) that included, from left to right, Yvonne Azeff, Tammy Holz, and Bryan Beccia.

Trainer Nancy Alberts (top) saddled Maryland hero Magic Weisner to a near upset, at odds of 45-1, in the 2002 Preakness Stakes. Magic Weisner (left) finished second to Derby victor War Emblem.

War Emblem's exercise rider Mick Jenner (above left) was dating Hanne Jorgensen (right), assistant to trainer Ken McPeek, during the 2002 Triple Crown races. McPeek's Sarava (top left) derailed War Emblem's Belmont bid.

Smarty Jones earned the affections of Philadelphians when he won the 2004 Kentucky Derby. Fans came in droves to see him work out at Philadelphia Park (left) and wished him well en route to Belmont Park.

Afleet Alex went to his knees in the 2005 Preakness before humbling his competition. He annexed two-thirds of the Triple Crown with a decisive score in the Belmont Stakes.

After his breathtaking Kentucky Derby victory, Barbaro returned to his base of Fair Hill in Maryland to launch his doomed Preakness bid.

Jim French (left) didn't win a Triple Crown race, but he didn't miss any dances.

Arts and Letters (top) thwarted Majestic Prince's Triple Crown bid in 1969 while Stage Door Johnny (above) did the same to Forward Pass in 1968.

about the city of Louisville, and I hope you come back next year, Mr. Pegram."

Pegram replied, "First off, you can call me Mike, and I'll be back."

After dropping Pegram off at the barn, Thompson told him, "The next time I see you will be when you win the Kentucky Derby."

A month later Pegram flew with Baffert and Silver Charm to New York for the gray colt's attempt to sweep the Triple Crown.

As they sat on an ice chest in the front of the plane, Pegram said to Baffert, "One thing about all this. I might never get this far myself, but at least I know what it feels like to go through the Triple Crown."

Pegram did get that far himself the following year. As if written for a movie, Pegram's colt, Real Quiet, captured the 1998 Kentucky Derby, and after the race, who was waiting to escort him to the winner's circle? Steve Thompson, whose words to Pegram the previous year had proved eerily prophetic. Not many people can say the same police officer escorted them out of jail and, a year later, into the winner's circle of the Kentucky Derby.

Real Quiet went on to win the Preakness Stakes and headed to Belmont to try and become racing's twelfth Triple Crown winner. But the movie script did not end in typical Hollywood fashion as Real Quiet suffered a heartbreaking nose defeat in the Belmont Stakes at the hands of Victory Gallop, whom he had beaten in the

Derby and Preakness.

Pegram and Thompson became good friends, visiting each other often. Two years later Pegram was back at the Kentucky Derby with a colt he had named Captain Steve after his new friend.

Thompson was now a cult hero in Louisville. As he walked with his namesake from the barn to the paddock, the crowd cheered wildly for him. He waved back, thrusting his arms in the air and shouting "we're gonna win this for the regular folks."

Captain Steve could only manage an eighth-place finish but came back two weeks later to finish fourth in the Preakness Stakes. The following year he captured the richest race in the world, the $6 million Dubai World Cup. With grade I victories in the Swaps Stakes, Donn Handicap, and Hollywood Futurity, Captain Steve earned nearly $7 million for Pegram.

But to Thompson, the whole experience meant a lot more than money.

"What means the most to me is the friendship of Mike, the love of the horse, and the love of the game," he said. "This has all been one fairy tale."

13

From Cheers to Tears (2000)

In the world of Thoroughbred racing, joy and heartache alternate on a daily, even hourly, basis. The exultation of victory lasts only until a horse's next defeat or injury. These conflicting emotions are magnified during the Triple Crown, where immortality can be achieved in a matter of minutes, sometimes seconds, and dictated by the bob of a nose.

Exercise rider Andy Durnin's emotional ride through the 2000 Triple Crown went far beyond winning and losing.

Originally, Durnin was not even part of the Triple Crown scene that year. When trainer Neil Drysdale sent Kentucky Derby favorite Fusaichi Pegasus to Churchill Downs to prepare for the Run for the Roses following the colt's impressive victory in the Wood Memorial at Aqueduct, Durnin was in California exercising horses for his good friend Eddie Gregson.

Several years earlier Drysdale had recruited Durnin to help tame the savage beast in one of his top horses, Labeeb, who was a basket case on the racetrack, often ducking out badly during a race. With Durnin's help in the mornings — his strength and his ability to get horses to respond to him — Labeeb was able to win a number of major stakes and finish third in the Breeders' Cup Mile in his final career start.

Just prior to the 2000 Kentucky Derby, trainer Beau Greely asked Durnin to accompany him and his grass star Manndar to Churchill Downs, where the horse was scheduled to run in the Woodford Reserve Turf Classic, the race before the Derby.

After getting Gregson's permission, Durnin agreed.

Drysdale, meanwhile, had his hands full with Fusaichi Pegasus, a grand-looking colt with an enormous stride and an untapped amount of talent. However, the colt had a few mental issues. He was high strung and unpredictable, doing what was asked only when he felt like it and rearing without warning or provocation.

Right before the Wood Memorial, as the horses circled behind the gate preparing to load, one horse was missing. Binoculars scoured the entire Aqueduct stretch in search of the bright red-and-yellow silks of Fusaichi Pegasus' owner, Fusao Sekiguchi. But they were nowhere to be found.

Finally, off in the distance, near the five-sixteenths pole, the colt was spotted standing like the proverbial statue, his feet planted firmly on the ground. "Come on, big boy, we gotta go," his jockey Kent Desormeaux pleaded to no avail. The Wood Memorial at that moment was the furthest thing from Fusaichi Pegasus' mind. His only interest seemed to be checking out all the buses and cars in the parking lot.

In an attempt to get the colt's mind back on the race, one of the gate crew ran up the track, grabbed hold of the bridle, and tried to coax him into going by running alongside him. That worked until the colt decided to stop near the eighth pole and gawk at the crowd. By the time the outrider showed up to assist, Fusaichi Pegasus was ready, and he obligingly jogged alongside the pony to the gate, where he proceeded to walk in as if nothing had happened.

Preparing for the Derby, Drysdale took the talented hopeful out under the cover of darkness, as soon as the track opened for training. One morning following his gallop, a little more than a week before the race, Fusaichi Pegasus was walking back along the rail under his regular exercise rider, Nuno Santos, when out of nowhere he reared straight up. Instead of coming down on all fours as would any other horse, he went straight down on his rear end and basically sat on the track in an upright position. With no way to stay on top of the horse, Santos slid right off the colt's back.

Now riderless, Fusaichi Pegasus scrambled to his feet, and before he had a chance even to think about running off, Drysdale raced onto the track and grabbed the reins.

The next day an exasperated Drysdale once again summoned his top troubleshooter, Durnin, who had arrived at Churchill Downs with Manndar. Durnin had worked Fusaichi Pegasus before the Wood and was familiar with the temperamental colt.

Fusaichi Pegasus was a perfect gentleman from the first morning that Durnin climbed aboard. His riding style fit perfectly with Fusaichi Pegasus as it had with Labeeb, and the colt responded. Each morning after training, Drysdale would turn Fusaichi Pegasus loose in D. Wayne Lukas' sandpen behind the barn, where the colt would put on a show — jumping, bucking, and rearing for all those watching.

On the first Saturday in May, Durnin had one of those days people can only dream about. First, he watched Manndar win the Woodford Reserve as the 5-1 fourth choice, and a race later he experienced the ultimate thrill when Fusaichi Pegasus became the first favorite to win the Kentucky Derby since Spectacular Bid twenty-one years earlier.

Following the winner's circle photo, Durnin waved to the cheering crowd as he led Fusaichi Pegasus back to the test barn.

Still unable to believe what had just happened, Durnin could barely hear his cell phone faintly ringing through the roar of the crowd. On the other end was his close friend Craig Quinn, calling from South Carolina to congratulate him.

"How are you, my brother?" Durnin asked in his

distinct Irish accent. "I'm just walking back to the stables with the Kentucky Derby winner. How about that? Did you see Manndar win the race before? That's the only reason I'm even here. This is the best day of my life."

But Durnin's joy would be short-lived. Four weeks later he experienced one of the worst days of his life.

After arriving at Belmont for the Belmont Stakes, I spotted Durnin leaning against his car outside Barn 4. The bottle of water he held in his hand was shaking noticeably. His boss, Eddie Gregson, had committed suicide the day before. As much as Durnin tried, he couldn't hold back his tears as he searched for the right words to describe the way he felt about his close friend.

He had received the call in the middle of the night from fellow exercise rider and friend Jimmy Duggan, who had been filling in for him during his Triple Crown odyssey.

A month earlier Durnin had been sitting atop a Kentucky Derby winner, but now his entire world had been turned upside down. Fusaichi Pegasus had been beaten on an off track in the Preakness and had injured his foot in his stall, forcing him to miss the Belmont. Durnin still had Manndar, who was pointing for the Manhattan Handicap, and Belmont Stakes longshot Hugh Hefner for trainer Marty Jones, but it seemed insignificant compared to the devastating loss of one of the most important people in his life.

Durnin and Gregson had been much more than exercise rider and trainer; they were close friends who would often have dinner and drinks together.

"When I was in the hospital after falling off one of Eddie's horses, I woke up from unconsciousness and there was a bottle of Dom Perignon [champagne] sitting there beside me," Durnin said. "That's the kind of guy Eddie was."

It was Gregson who had given Durnin his blessing when the rider asked permission to go to Kentucky with Greely and Manndar. Gregson was familiar with Triple Crown glory, having won the 1982 Kentucky Derby with Gato Del Sol.

Following the Derby, Durnin had returned to California and asked Gregson for permission to continue through the Triple Crown. Gregson gave him a hug and said, "Run with it. Enjoy the ride."

"He was laughing his ass off," Durnin said. "That was the last time I ever saw him."

What made the news even more difficult was that eighteen years earlier in Ireland, when Durnin was only seventeen, his brother had been found lying on the pavement next to a hotel on Christmas Eve.

"Someone evidently threw him off the roof, but I never knew any of the details," Durnin said. "I couldn't bring myself to ask my parents, and I haven't to this day. It's just too painful to ask. That was the most pain I ever felt in my life, but this one is just as bad."

But Durnin's emotional roller-coaster ride wasn't over. On Belmont day Manndar won the Manhattan Handicap with a spectacular stretch run. Again a part of the winner's circle ceremony, he found it hard to take Gregson's advice to enjoy the ride, but he was happy for Manndar and took solace in the joy the victory brought Greely.

As much as he hurt, he was able, for a short while, to feel good about something. As he walked alone through the tunnel to the backstretch following the race, I asked him if Manndar's victory helped relieve some of the pain.

"Big time," he said, as the tears began to well up. "Big time."

14

Operation Derby (2001)

The stable of horses trained by John Ward Jr. that arrived at Churchill Downs in the early spring of 2001 was similar to any other top stable, except it was run by a handpicked team whose specific goal was to win the Kentucky Derby.

Ward, with his wife, Donna, has for years maintained a private stable and farm across the road from the back entrance to Keeneland Race Course. The couple trains a large stable of horses there, 95 percent of which are owned by John and Debby Oxley.

In December 2000, when the Wards headed to Florida, they had three top-class three-year-olds that looked to be serious Derby horses. Holiday Thunder had finished second in the Kentucky Cup Juvenile at Turfway Park behind Point Given, second in the Kentucky Jockey Club Stakes at Churchill Downs, and third in the Breeders'

Futurity at Keeneland. Hero's Tribute had finished second, beaten a neck, in the Iroquois Stakes at Churchill Downs. And the bottom horse on the totem pole, Monarchos, had come from the clouds to finish a promising third in a maiden race at Churchill Downs and was only several weeks away from another maiden race.

The Wards had their two-year-olds and older horses stabled at Palm Beach Downs, but they felt their three big horses, ready to embark on the Derby trail, would be better off stabled at Gulfstream Park. So, they decided to set up another division that would concentrate strictly on the Derby preps. The first thing they did was assemble a team with what Ward called the "big-day experience." In basketball terms, they wanted people who wouldn't "freeze up on the foul line."

They began by hiring Yvonne Azeff to run the barn. John had been trying to hire Azeff for years. She had been an assistant to Pat Byrne when he won the Breeders' Cup Classic with Awesome Again, and she had been an assistant to D. Wayne Lukas when he won the Classic with Cat Thief. Azeff was no-nonsense when it came to horses, and she could train and organize a stable with the best of them.

At age thirteen she had ridden her bike to Bowie Racetrack in Maryland and snuck into the backstretch through a hole in the fence to be around the horses. Even then, her life's dream, like that of so many other horse lovers, was one day to win the Kentucky Derby.

Azeff began riding at tracks around the country and

was the leading apprentice rider at Tampa Bay Downs in 1992. But training was her passion, and she was able to prove her ability running a stable by working for some of the top trainers in the country. She was everything Ward was looking for, and now he had the lure of Derby fever to entice her.

After hiring Azeff, he allowed her to go out and recruit her own team of assistants, exercise riders, grooms, and hotwalkers.

The Wards then selected some twelve horses, including Holiday Thunder, Hero's Tribute, and Monarchos, whom they would send to Gulfstream Park and later, following the Florida Derby, right on to Churchill Downs. One of them caught Azeff's attention immediately. While still at Palm Beach Downs, before setting up shop at Gulfstream, she took a liking to Monarchos, a son of Maria's Mon, sensing something special about him.

"John, am I going to get this little gray colt?" she asked. "I think he's going to be a star."

One day at Gulfstream Azeff saw a friend, Bob Lewis, walking out in the rain and approached him about working with her. Lewis had worked as an assistant to Carl Nafzger for ten years and before that as an assistant to Lou Rondinello, who had the powerful Darby Dan horses.

"I've got a job for you that you cannot refuse," Azeff told him.

The money she offered him far surpassed what he had been making. Lewis had known Azeff for a long time and respected her as a horsewoman. After working for Darby Dan, Lewis had gone back to school and eventually got a job trading commodities for Barnett Bank in Florida. But the job was a pressure cooker, and after six years he felt he had to get out. He returned to the racetrack, took a job with Nafzger, and was around such stars as Travers Stakes winner Unshaded and champion three-year-old filly Banshee Breeze.

So, Azeff had her assistant. When another friend of hers, Tammy Holtz, who had worked as a groom for Azeff, heard about the new all-star team of horses and people being assembled, she contacted Azeff, who hired her as groom in January 2001. Holtz was born and raised on a wheat farm in northeast Oregon. After graduating high school, she packed her bags, got in her car, and drove to Louisville to look for work. She began walking hots for Jack Van Berg in 1988 and graduated to groom. She then spent seven years with Nafzger, taking over as Unbridled's groom following the Triple Crown. Now, she had an opportunity to return.

Also joining the team were exercise rider Bryan Beccia, hotwalkers Teri Upton and Mike Jackson, and a number of other qualified horse people. Everything was in place. It was on to the Kentucky Derby trail.

Azeff gave Holtz Monarchos to rub and put Beccia up as regular exercise rider. What everyone in the barn liked about Holtz was her even temperament. Nothing seemed to bother her. Once Monarchos took a liking to her, the two became good friends, and Holtz would stop on her way to the track in the afternoon and buy carrots and apples for him. Monarchos took a lot of patient handling. He could get keyed up over little things, such as rain dripping on the awning.

But the one thing he had going for him, in addition to his talent, was his assertiveness and intelligence. When he was born, his mother, Regal Band, jumped to her feet after giving birth, breaking the umbilical cord. Instead of lying there or getting up and wobbling around the stall on shaky legs like most foals, he jumped to his feet right with her and just stood there perfectly balanced on all fours. As a youngster, he never got sick or even had as much as a scratch. He was the dominant colt of the group but never had to fight to establish leadership. Because of his exuberant personality, Azeff nicknamed him Sparky.

On January 13, Monarchos won a seven-furlong maiden race by six lengths. Shortly afterward, Azeff called her mother, Barbara Barnhill, an accomplished horsewoman in her own right, and told her, "Mom, make your plans now to go to the Derby because we've got a shot to win with this gray colt we've got."

Three weeks later Monarchos stretched out 1 1/16 miles and easily won an allowance race by nearly five lengths. Then it was Hero's Tribute's turn, and he made his three-year-old debut a winning one, capturing a seven-furlong allowance race by four lengths in a snappy 1:22 1/5.

During this time, Azeff, Holtz, and Beccia noticed that Monarchos had started doing a little dance step, the "Sparky Shuffle," while going to the track. He would normally do this right before a race, when he was feeling good and ready for battle. The way Azeff described it, he would swish his tail and "shift his ass" a few times and then throw in a little buck and a half kick.

On February 17, Holiday Thunder made his three-year-old debut in the Fountain of Youth Stakes but turned in a terrible effort, finishing a well-beaten sixth. An injury suffered in the race knocked the colt off the Derby trail. And then there were two.

March 10 and 11 would be the Wards' make-or-break weekend, with Monarchos running in the Florida Derby on Saturday and Hero's Tribute going to Fair Grounds for the following day's Louisiana Derby. This would determine whether all the work of assembling this new team and stable was worth the time and expense.

The Florida Derby drew thirteen horses, and down the backstretch and approaching the far turn, Monarchos had only two horses behind him. Then, as they rounded the far turn, jockey Jorge Chavez pulled the trigger on Sparky, and the result was a move so explosive that no one could recall seeing anything like it in a Derby prep. Monarchos flew past the ten horses in front of him with a breathtaking, sweeping move.

By the time they hit the top of the stretch, Monarchos was already in front, and he continued to pour it on, winning by 4½ lengths. Just like that, the Derby had an exciting star to challenge Point Given, Bob Baffert's towering one-horse wrecking crew, who was everyone's choice to win the Run for the Roses.

Hero's Tribute finished a decent third in the Louisiana Derby, but a poor effort in the subsequent Blue Grass Stakes at Keeneland, in which he suffered from a thyroid problem, knocked him off the Derby trail as well. Now there was one. But what a one that was.

Ward decided to use the Wood Memorial as Monarchos' final Derby prep. A lot was now expected of the colt, but Ward realized he would have his hands full going against Baffert's other big colt, the rising star Congaree. The last thing Ward wanted was another monster effort like the one in the Florida Derby and to have Monarchos bust a gut trying to run down the speedy Congaree. So, when Monarchos finished a solid second to Congaree, who was in complete control of the race all the way, Ward was happy. Others, who thought Monarchos was some kind of super horse after the Florida Derby, weren't as upbeat as Ward over his defeat.

Now, it was back to Churchill Downs, where Monarchos and company had been since March 26. Donna spent almost every day at Keeneland taking care of her horses while John would work with the newly arrived two-year-olds, occasionally coming to Churchill to check on Monarchos and Hero's Tribute and the other horses in the barn. He had complete faith in Azeff, who would map out the daily schedules and give instructions to the riders.

She also brought in a friend of hers, Diane Volz, an equine physical therapist, to work on Monarchos, who had a tendency to get stiff behind. One morning Baffert had watched Monarchos gallop by and commented,

"Man, that's a stiff-going sonofabitch." The second time past the stands, however, Monarchos had worked out the stiffness. "He's moving better now," Baffert said.

Meanwhile, many began to feel that Monarchos was going in the wrong direction, especially when Ward opted to give the colt several days off, keeping him in the barn and just walking the shed. That always sends up a red flag to the media, who question any day off by a Derby horse. But Ward had written a script for the Derby, starting back in December, and he wasn't about to go against what his years of experience were telling him.

Monarchos had trained exceptionally well since arriving at Churchill Downs in March, and with his spectacular performance in the Florida Derby and second in the Wood Memorial, as well as another 1⅛-mile race under his belt, Ward thought he deserved an occasional day off.

Ward also went against tradition when he gave Monarchos his final Derby work eight days before the race. The day before, when asked what kind of work he was looking for, Ward stated emphatically that Monarchos would work five furlongs between 1:00 and 1:01, gallop out six furlongs in about 1:14, and pull up in seven furlongs in about 1:28.

The following morning he punched his desired times into his gray computer and just waited for it to print out. Monarchos went out with Beccia aboard and worked five furlongs in 1:00⅘, galloping out in 1:14⅕ and pulling up in 1:28⅕. Ward couldn't have programmed it any better.

After several days off, Monarchos was back in training.

Azeff started getting confident when she saw the colt doing the old Sparky Shuffle again. As he came off the track, she and Beccia looked at each other and smiled. They didn't have to say a word. They knew what was coming.

Two days before the Derby, Ward showed up from Lexington to watch Monarchos gallop and school at the gate, driving his SUV through the tunnel into the infield. He had discovered that the best place to watch Monarchos train was atop one of the new luxury suites. Watching from an elevated position inside the rail provided him with a clear, panoramic view of the entire track. He climbed up the steps to the awning-covered balcony and just soaked up the view, as a warm summer-like breeze blew his sandy blonde hair. Watching Monarchos gallop and school was an even better tonic. The colt rolled around the track at a strong clip, his legs reaching out for more ground. He wanted to do more, and it took Beccia an extra furlong to persuade him the morning chores were finally over.

"Look at him," Ward said. "He's mentally bright and sound. He really wants to mix it up. That's just what I was looking for."

When Monarchos returned to the barn, a beaming Beccia told Azeff she needn't worry about Point Given, the massive chestnut who had romped in the Santa Anita Derby and San Felipe Stakes.

"We're ready for 'em," he said. "They won't beat us. Don't let that big red sonofabitch stumble or we might run right over top of him."

The unseasonably warm temperatures continued into Derby Day. Monarchos began to get a bit hot walking over to the paddock, but as he stood in the saddling stall, Azeff could feel him already cooling off. When Chavez mounted the colt, people began shouting, "Go get 'em, Georgie," but Monarchos never turned a hair. Azeff looked up at Chavez and said, "He's dialed in today."

History will show that Monarchos blew the 127th Kentucky Derby wide open, winning by nearly five lengths. His final time of 1:59⅘ was the second-fastest Derby ever run. Only Secretariat's track-record time of 1:59⅖ was faster.

Azeff ran on to the track, sobbing uncontrollably, her face buried in her hands. "Oh, my God," she kept repeating. Beccia came running over to her from the opposite direction and the two embraced. "We got it," he said.

Azeff then hugged her mother, who seemed in a daze, as if trying to still absorb what had just happened. When her mother returned to the barn a short while later, she sat down on a chair and just stared off into space.

"I'm numb just thinking about all those years and all the sacrifices," she said. "Yvonne is married to the job and to the horses. You have no idea the sacrifices she's made in her personal life to get to where she is today. Now it's all paid off. I can't keep from crying. I'm still shaking."

For Bob Lewis, who watched the race on TV in the tack room, it was his own personal Triple Crown, having been assistant trainer in 1974 when Little Current won the

Preakness and Belmont stakes for Darby Dan.

"It was a wild scene in the room," he said. "Everyone was trying to jump on everybody else."

Ward, however, remained calm, as if he had this moment all planned out — and in a way he had. He had written the script to this year's Kentucky Derby and then watched as the players read each and every line to perfection. The third-generation Kentucky horseman had made his family proud. He had won racing's ultimate prize with the ghosts of his noted ancestors looking down on him. Most important, he showed what planning, horsemanship, and patience could accomplish.

But the glory would be short-lived. This would be the final hurrah for Ward's elite team, and for Monarchos himself. The colt ran a disappointing race in the Preakness, finishing sixth behind the victorious Point Given. Brought back in the Belmont, he finished third, but was beaten thirteen lengths by Point Given, who took over as the country's leading three-year-old.

A short while later a hairline fracture was discovered in Monarchos' right front knee. Everyone agreed the fracture had actually begun in the Kentucky Derby over a lightning-fast track, and the colt had been running on it in the Preakness and Belmont, which accounted for his poor performances.

Another seven months passed before Monarchos made it back to the races. He returned with a dull third-place finish in an allowance/optional claiming race at Gulfstream Park but came out of the race with an injury to the left front medial branch of the superficial digital flexor tendon. He was retired to Claiborne Farm in Paris, Kentucky.

When the Triple Crown ended, many members of Ward's Derby team went their separate ways. Azeff remained and took Ward's string to Gulfstream Park the following winter. On January 26, 2002, she was on the stable pony, Mouse, who had become a valuable member of the barn and a constant companion to Monarchos.

They were ponying a particularly tough horse, and as they were coming off the track, the horse lunged sharply into Mouse, who jumped in the air and lost his balance. He fell over backward, throwing Azeff and pinning her against a fence.

She suffered a severe injury to her brain stem that left her in a coma for twenty-seven days. When she slowly came out of it, all she was able to do was move her eyes and occasionally utter a word or two. She was unable to hold her neck up or breathe properly, requiring a tracheotomy, nor could she swallow or eat. The prognosis by the neurosurgeon was that she most likely was going to be "a vegetable."

When she was transferred from Hollywood Memorial Regional Hospital to Pinecrest Rehabilitation Hospital, she arrived with tubes in her stomach and a bad staph infection. She also had no use of her right arm, having torn her rotator cuff in the fall. With little coordination, she had to learn how to eat.

But she became an inspiration to all the physical

therapists at Pinecrest because of her incredible drive. She soon began to show dramatic improvement. When Ward came to visit, the first thing she said to him was, "Boss, I can be ready in two weeks. You didn't take it out on Mouse, did you? It wasn't his fault."

She would remain at Pinecrest another three months, staring constantly at a photo of Monarchos as her own inspiration. That spring, after being released, she visited Monarchos at Claiborne Farm. She had to use a walker to get around, which concerned the farm help as she approached the stallion. But Monarchos stood right next to her and, to the amazement of everyone watching, began licking her from her feet to her head.

Still having problems with her equilibrium and with controlling her temper, a result of the head injury that required therapy, she returned to work at Ward's barn, leaving her Louisville house at 3:30 in the morning for the seventy-mile drive to Lexington.

But she was unable to maintain that pace or remain on the job and was out of work for a long while. But she now is in Florida clocking horses at Palm Meadows and taking courses in physical therapy.

"I keep her in my prayers," Lewis said.

As for Beccia, he was unable to deal with a severe drug problem, and after several arrests and convictions on drug- and alcohol-related charges, he was convicted of manufacturing, trafficking, and being in possession of methamphetamine and was sentenced to twenty-five years in prison. His wife, jockey Greta Kuntzweiler, whom he had married in 2005, also was convicted on drug charges and was sentenced to five years probation.

Lewis left racing when a friend began having financial problems with his company and needed Lewis' expertise to help save his business. It took Lewis four years to restructure the company and get it straightened out so that it was in a comfortable financial position. He then returned to the racetrack and once again is working for Ward.

Holtz also left Ward, and currently is walking hots at Keeneland in the mornings and working in the garden shop at Wal-Mart in the afternoons.

Mouse, who had been performing in rodeos when Ward bought him, was retired to the Wards' farm in 2004, where his new job is serving as "baby sitter" to the weanlings.

The team that Ward assembled did not last long, but for that one special season, they were able to work together to win America's greatest race.

As Ward said, "It was set up for one goal. We had one target, and everybody did what they were supposed to do. It just goes to show you, in this business it's all about the chemistry among the people you have working for you."

And if there was one thing Ward's team had it was chemistry, and one talented gray horse.

15

Magic in Maryland
(2002)

One of the most fascinating personalities I've met on the Triple Crown trail is trainer Nancy Alberts, who nearly pulled off a shocker in the 2002 Preakness Stakes with 45-1 shot Magic Weisner, a feat that would have ranked among the great Cinderella stories in Triple Crown history.

Alberts owned, bred, and trained "Magic," as he was known, and saw him rise from the $40,000 maiden claiming ranks to finish second in a classic and then win the Ohio Derby and finish second in the Haskell Invitational Handicap. But the story of Magic Weisner would continue well after those summer three-year-old races.

A small-time veteran Maryland horsewoman, Alberts was born in the horse country of southeast Pennsylvania, near West Chester, and rode horses over the jumps.

Her first horse was a former racehorse that someone had given to the local hunt club to feed to the hounds because one of the horse's hips was lower than the other. But Alberts bought him for $200 and began working with him, teaching him to become a successful jumper.

After working as an assistant for trainer James P. Simpson for twenty years, Alberts went out on her own and ran a modest stable at Laurel, keeping anywhere from fifteen to twenty horses. She became hardened by the racetrack, especially having to endure those long, cold Maryland winters.

When she wasn't training and taking care of her horses, she was repairing horse blankets, making nosebands (shadow rolls), and clipping horses. According to those close to her, Alberts clipped half the horses stabled at Laurel. And she was always available to van any horse.

It was only appropriate that a horse such as Magic Weisner should come her way. A son of Ameri Valay, he was produced by Alberts' mare Jazema, whom she had bought from her old boss, James Simpson, for a dollar. Magic Weisner was just another horse when he was being broken by Ron Houghton. But he kept improving, and after escaping from his career debut without being claimed, he continued moving up the ladder. Ironically, he was sent off at odds of 45-1 in his debut, the same odds he would go off at in the Preakness.

He won six of seven races, including four stakes, before finishing second as the 4-5 favorite in the Federico Tesio Stakes at Pimlico a month before the Preakness.

Earlier in the year David Rollinson, racing secretary at Pimlico and Laurel, had called Alberts to tell her she should nominate Magic Weisner to the Triple Crown, which cost only $600 at that stage. She happily put up the money.

The Tesio was the last stop before the Preakness, and there was no reason to think Magic Weisner wouldn't add the race to his growing list of stakes wins.

Before the race Alberts, who was nursing a broken shoulder at the time, gave jockey Phil Teator explicit instructions.

"Pimlico is a lot different than Laurel, so you have to stay up close. You can't let them get away from you," she told him.

Soon after the start, Teator took Magic Weisner back to fifth. The gelding closed well but fell two lengths short.

"You blew the race," a disgusted Alberts told Teator.

Despite the defeat, she decided to continue her quest for the Preakness, but with another rider. It just so happened that the jockey who rode the Tesio winner, New York-based Richard Migliore, heard that Alberts was looking for a rider and had his agent call her. He was going to be at Pimlico anyway to ride a race on the undercard, so this was an opportunity to get a Preakness mount even though the horse would be one of the longest prices in the field.

On Preakness morning Alberts put Magic Weisner in a small horse trailer and drove him up to Pimlico, arriving late morning.

The pace in the Preakness was brisk, with Kentucky Derby winner War Emblem tracking longshot Menacing Dennis. Migliore, meanwhile, had Magic Weisner back in eleventh in the thirteen-horse field. Passing the five-sixteenths pole, War Emblem shot to the lead and began to open up on the field. Derby runner-up Proud Citizen moved up to challenge, but War Emblem found another gear and opened up again.

Just when everyone thought this would be another dominating victory for War Emblem, here came Magic Weisner flying out in the middle of the track. The home crowd erupted, hoping to see their hero pull off one of the great upsets in Triple Crown history. For a split second it looked as if it could happen, but Magic Weisner simply ran out of ground, falling three-quarters of a length short.

Alberts had nearly won the Preakness with a non-descript homebred and former claimer whose dam she had purchased for a dollar. The Baltimore and Washington newspapers and TV stations gave Magic Weisner almost as much ink and air time as they did the winner.

Now, it was on to the Belmont Stakes, although Alberts knew that the 1½-mile distance was stretching it for Magic. Unlike the Preakness, where they remained secluded at Laurel and well under the radar, she and Magic were now a hot story, and as soon as they arrived at Belmont, the media lined up outside her barn looking for a good underdog story to fill their copy.

"We're just going to save ground and run our own race," she said. "This is a big racetrack, and we don't want to make a move until we turn for home."

Magic Weisner sat back in sixth most of the race and although he couldn't threaten the first two finishers, Sarava and Medaglia d'Oro, he managed to finish fourth. War Emblem, who stumbled badly at the start, wound up eighth.

Magic would continue to prove that he was a top-class horse by winning the Ohio Derby and finishing a solid second behind War Emblem in the Haskell Invitational. But, just when everything seemed to being going perfectly, it all fell apart.

After the Haskell, Magic came down with a 102-degree temperature. He began exhibiting neurological problems and was sent to New Bolton Medical Center in West Chester, Pennsylvania, where it was discovered he was suffering from West Nile virus. The other two horses in Maryland that came down with West Nile died. Alberts learned that the disease claims the lives of 40 percent of the horses that contract it.

"When he walked around the barn, he'd fall down," Alberts said. "His brain swelled up, and he was in so much pain you couldn't even touch his head. He looked and acted like he had a severe headache. And what it did was pinch some of the nerves that go to his right hind end, and his whole hip had muscle atrophy in it.

"It was horrible to have to see him suffer like that. He's such a good, honest horse, he didn't deserve to suffer. All

I could do was make him as comfortable as I could. It was just so sad to see."

Magic Weisner was administered butazolidan and banamine to relieve the pain and inflammation, then put on Neigh-Lox to avoid gastritis from the medication.

In November, Alberts sent him to John Salzman's farm to continue his recovery. He returned to Alberts' barn at Laurel in early January and had his first work in mid-February. But by May he still wasn't right, and Alberts backed off on his training and hired an acupuncturist. He began to show immediate improvement and soon was back working. When Magic began to show some of that old spark, Alberts started looking for a race.

"He doesn't seem quite as racy as he did last year, but maybe a race will wake him up." Alberts said at the time. "He's been through so much, and he's come a long way. It's hard to believe it's been just about one year since the Haskell. It doesn't seem possible."

In May 2005 Alberts abandoned all hope of a comeback and announced Magic's retirement.

"I decided a couple weeks ago when I worked him against this filly [Rudy's Dee Dee] who is the slowest filly in my barn, and she whipped him from the gate," Alberts said. "He tried. He just didn't have the power in the hind end to push off.

"He looks fine, but the West Nile virus just damaged all the nerves, I'm sure he'll be able to have another profession. He's at the farm, just trying to get the fitness out of him. I've had a couple people contact me about making him a dressage horse. He is a beautiful mover and sound and loves to do anything."

So, with seven victories from fifteen starts, including five stakes wins, and earnings of $888,830, Magic Weisner was retired.

"I'm still proud of him," said Alberts. "Even now, he knows he is special."

So is Alberts, who matches her horse in toughness and durability. At the end of 2002, Alberts earned a special achievement award from the Maryland Thoroughbred Horsemen's Association and was named the Honorary Postmaster for the 2003 Preakness.

Alberts' greatest admirer is her son, Will, a senior systems engineer at the Pentagon. Will provided Alberts with her greatest victory when she learned he had survived the terrorist attack on the Pentagon on September, 11, 2001.

"I've worked hard in my life, but I'm humbled by her," Will said several years ago. "Simply put, nobody works harder than her, and believe me, she has no interest in glory and fame. She just loves what she does.

"She's out there at 4:30 every morning, and then she goes to two different farms to take care of the weanlings and yearlings. Then she returns to the track to feed the horses. Then she goes back to the farms to feed the babies. She does this every day of the year, with no help. She takes so much pride in her work, and she'll never half-ass anything.

"Yes, she deserves what she's gotten with Magic

Weisner, but she doesn't want the spotlight. She just loves taking pride in the horses she bred and raised, the same way a parent takes pride in their children. The horses are her kids now.

"And she does all this despite her physical ailments. She has shingles all along the left side of her upper torso that really bother her. She has lower back problems. The back of her arm has severe nerve damage. And she suffered a broken left shoulder two weeks before Magic Weisner's Preakness. Even shortly after she gave birth to me she wound up breaking her collarbone. She's like a machine. She just keeps going and doesn't let anything stop her."

Will had said at the time the biggest reward his mother could have would not be to win the Kentucky Derby or the Preakness, it would be to find her own farm near the racetrack, instead of having to lease other people's farms.

"Her dream is to wake up in the morning and look out the window and see her babies playing in the field," he said.

That dream came true in December 2003, when she finally was able buy a farm of her own. She kept Magic Weisner there for several years, but when he began getting bored, she sent him to her sister and her boyfriend's farm in West Chester, Pennsylvania, where, at age nine, he is being ridden in cross-country events with the Radnor Hunt Club. Alberts said he's getting adept at his new lifestyle and is taking to it "like a champ."

They expect him soon to be participating in fox hunts.

In 2006, Alberts saddled Magic's brother, Diamond David, to a second-place finish in the $237,500 Maryland Million Classic at odds of 21-1.

The following year, the purse increased to $300,000, which lured better quality horses from New York and other nearby tracks. Although Diamond David was overmatched even more than he had been the previous year, Alberts tried again and Diamond David managed to finish third at odds of 43-1.

In her typical manner, she said on the eve of the race, "That's OK, we'll just have to get tough."

16

In Love and War
(2002)

No one paid much attention when Sarava and assistant trainer Hanne Jorgensen arrived at Belmont Park ten days before the 2002 Belmont Stakes. Jorgensen, an assistant to trainer Kenny McPeek, accompanied the colt from their home base at Churchill Downs, serving as his groom, exercise rider, and hotwalker.

There wouldn't be much buzz at Belmont until the Wednesday before the big race when Kentucky Derby and Preakness winner War Emblem was scheduled to arrive. The near-black colt, whom Bob Baffert purchased for slightly less than a million dollars for Prince Ahmed Salman's the Thoroughbred Corporation three weeks before the Derby, would be the trainer's third horse in six years to try to sweep the Triple Crown.

War Emblem's regular exercise rider, Mick Jenner, just happened to be Jorgensen's boyfriend, making for an interesting dynamic. If there was any competition between the two, it was lighthearted and friendly. The reason was simple: War Emblem was the best three-year-old in the country and on the threshold of immortality while no one was taking Sarava, one of the longest-priced horses in the race, seriously. Because their expectations were on such different levels, Jorgensen and Jenner could afford to kid around about their upcoming meeting.

Jorgensen was born in Oslo, Norway. She was introduced to horses at age three by her father's best friend, who was a trainer in France and Germany. She began riding in amateur races when she was fifteen and continued until she was twenty-two, competing in Fegentri (Federation of Gentlemen Riders) races all over Europe. She then rode professionally for two years but was not successful, so she turned her attention to training. After spending some time in America in 1993, she returned to the States for good in 1999 and went to work as an assistant to trainer Randy Morse, who brought her to Kentucky and taught her the administrative end of the sport.

After two years with Morse, she was hired by Helen Pitts, McPeek's assistant, who needed a top exercise rider. When Pitts traveled with the horses, Jorgensen ran the barn in her absence, and then it was Jorgensen who would do the traveling while Pitts stayed home. During her time with Pitts, Jorgensen took out her assistant trainer's license.

In 2002 she was given her first big break when McPeek had her take Sarava to New York for the Belmont. The son of Wild Again had begun his career in England before being sent to America in the fall of 2001. Following two races under trainer Burk Kessinger's care, he was turned over to McPeek. When Sarava captured the listed Sir Barton Stakes at Pimlico in his stakes debut on the Preakness undercard, McPeek immediately turned his attention to the 1½-mile Belmont, even though the colt had never raced farther than 1 1/16 miles.

Looking over War Emblem's competition in the Belmont, Jenner hadn't given Sarava a second thought. Perhaps Proud Citizen and Perfect Drift, the second- and third-place finishers in the Kentucky Derby, or Magic Weisner, the fast-closing runner-up in the Preakness, or even the talented Medaglia d'Oro and Sunday Break. Certainly not Sarava.

Jenner, an Army brat, was born in Germany and never lived in one place for more than six months. His parents' home was in Brighton, England, and he lived there on an off for eight years. He learned about horses through his father's commandant, a physical-training instructor attached with the cavalry. The commandant's wife taught him how to sit on a horse and trot, and he soon became an excellent rider. He began competing in steeplechase races in England and also was a skilled blacksmith, having worked for a farrier while in military school. He decided to stick with the horses, learning as much as he could about them, walking hots, feeding and clipping them, raking the yards, and taking the horses to the races.

While tending bar one afternoon, he received a phone call from a friend overseas, who was in Miami working for trainer Bill White. When Jenner found out his friend had a spare room, he told him he'd be there in two weeks. While in America, he dated trainer April Mayberry, daughter of trainer Brian Mayberry, and began breezing horses for her. He met Baffert and wound up exercising his top sprinter Thirty Slews, who would win the 1992 Breeders' Cup Sprint. Over the years Jenner would get on horses such as Silver Charm, Real Quiet, and Cavonnier for Baffert.

In the winter of 2000, Jenner met Jorgensen in a bar in Miami, and they began dancing to an ABBA song and talking for a while. Jenner remembered the meeting well, but Jorgensen, who admitted she probably wasn't too sober that night, had no recollection of it when Jenner walked into her barn at Churchill Downs one morning several months later and asked her out.

All she thought was, "At least people in Kentucky are friendly." She had no idea who this guy was and thought from his washed-out British accent that he was Australian. Jenner gave her his phone number and said to call him if she ever wanted to go out. A short while later she called and said, "Hey, take me to the movies." And they've been together ever since.

"Thank God she didn't remember me or she probably wouldn't have gone out with me," Jenner said.

In the spring of 2002, Jenner had been galloping horses at Keeneland for trainer Terry Oliver and working at the

Keeneland two-year-old sales when Baffert contacted him.

"Hey, I just bought a horse; you want to get on him?" Baffert said.

Jenner told him he was busy at the sales, but Baffert persisted.

"Just work it out, will you," he said. "I can't get anyone in California to come here and work this horse. You can get on him at 7:30 and then drive to Lexington in time to work with the sales horses."

Jenner had been in Ocala a few weeks earlier and had made it a point to watch the simulcast of the Illinois Derby. Jorgensen and Pitts were at Sportsman's Park to saddle their top-class three-year-old, Repent. Jenner knew Repent was a runner and couldn't believe it when War Emblem beat him by more than six lengths. Baffert, who had run out of Derby horses, bought War Emblem a few days later. When he contacted Jenner about riding him, the colt's reputation as a rogue and a nasty horse had already become well known. Jenner talked to riders who had been on or around him and they'd say, "He's a real sonofabitch when you have to back him up or turn him around." But rogue horses had never stopped Jenner before.

Jenner and War Emblem became quite a team, and the more he rode him the more special he felt the colt was. As the Belmont drew near, Jenner's confidence was sky high. The only question was harnessing the horse's incredible speed going 1½ miles.

Meanwhile, Jorgensen was going about her work with Sarava in relative quiet, as the only other Belmont starter on the grounds was the Bobby Frankel-trained Medaglia d'Oro.

The big three-year-old in the McPeek barn that spring had been Harlan's Holiday, who had won the Florida Derby and Blue Grass Stakes. Sent off as the lukewarm favorite in the Kentucky Derby, he finished seventh and then was a solid fourth in the Preakness. About a week before the Belmont, co-owner Jack Wolf informed McPeek the horse was being taken from him and given to Todd Pletcher. It was a crushing blow to the stable, but they had put to the loss behind them to concentrate on Sarava in the Belmont.

Each day Jorgensen could feel Sarava improving and getting stronger. She couldn't help but call Jenner and relay the news. At first, he'd listen, not really making much of it.

"You know what?" she told him. "You just might have a little competition on your hands."

And the more Sarava improved the more Jorgensen kept telling Jenner about it.

"Mick, this horse is really doing good," she'd say.

Finally, Jenner had heard enough.

"You gotta quit telling me this," he said to her. "Leave it alone already."

Jenner had enough on his mind. "We need everything to go our way for this horse to go a mile and a half," he said. "It's enough I have to worry about Medaglia d'Oro and the other horses. I don't need to hear her go on and on about this pot licker who's freakin' knee high to a grasshopper."

Once Jenner arrived at Belmont, however, they tried to keep the race at the track and not take it home with them. When he watched Sarava train, he admitted the colt had a shot to hit the board.

"We don't talk about it much at home," Jorgensen said at the time. "He does his job and I do mine, and we both wish each other well. We share each other's joys and sorrows. It's not up to us anyway; it's up to the horses. This isn't a hard situation for me personally because we're here as a longshot. Sarava is training super, and I'm hoping for the best. I'm just trying to back Mick up and build up his confidence. He's so in love with this horse, so you have to root for him to win the Triple Crown."

As race day neared, the tension at Baffert's barn began to build. He had been to the Belmont twice before, suffering heartbreaking defeats with Silver Charm and Real Quiet. He wanted this one badly. Jenner took a more philosophical approach.

"What am I going to worry about?" he said. "It's a horse race. The only thing I got to worry about is staying out of Baffert's way. He's a nervous sonofabitch. He seems to be OK now, so the Valium must be kicking in."

One morning before the race Jorgensen and McPeek were visited by Dawn Hayman, who claimed to be an "animal communicator." She said she was looking to have a "conversation" with one of the Belmont starters and hadn't had any luck with the other trainers.

"OK, well, give it a shot," McPeek told her.

First, Hayman "talked" to Sarava about having to leave his home at Churchill Downs, and she said he told her he missed the man there at night who would give him things from his pocket. Jorgensen then called the barn and had someone check with the night watchman, who said he always kept mints in his pocket and would feed them to Sarava every night.

Next, she asked him if he was feeling all right. She said Sarava told her, "I used to have a lot of pain on the inside of my right front foot, but that's fine now. The only things that bother me a little now are my heels, especially on my right side."

Jorgensen said that Sarava used to have a severe quarter crack on the inside of his right front foot, and now he had a slightly cracked heel on the right foot that gets sore on occasion. And during the winter he'd get a little muscle sore on his right side.

By this time Jorgensen was fascinated, knowing this woman could not have had any prior knowledge of these things.

"She could have read about the quarter crack somewhere, but that's all," Jorgensen said shortly after. "But she pinpointed it and said exactly where it was, and no one knew that except us. And there was no way she could have known about his heels bothering him."

"She really did connect with him," McPeek said. "The

fact that she knew about every little ailment gave her some legitimacy."

Hayman said Sarava also told her that he was not intimidated by other horses, but he didn't like being crowded too much, which is why he liked training at Belmont more than at Churchill Downs, which gets more crowded in the morning. She also said he told her he would go through a hole in a race if the rider asked him, but he needed help from the rider, he couldn't do it alone.

And, finally, when asked if he thought he was a good horse and could win the Belmont, Hayman said he answered, "I know I'm a good horse, and I just want the rest of the world to know. And I'm going to show them."

When the Allen Jerkens-trained Puzzlement was withdrawn from the Belmont a few days before the race, McPeek, a great admirer of the Hall of Fame trainer they called "the Giant Killer," expressed his regret about Jerkens' misfortune.

"Someday, I'd like to be 'the Giant Killer,' " McPeek said.

A few days later he would chop down Baffert's beanstalk.

A record crowd of 103,222 jammed Belmont to see whether War Emblem could do what no other horse had done in twenty-four years. Jorgensen remained quietly confident that Sarava would run a big race, and when the colt didn't turn a hair in the paddock, she began feeling good about his chances. The crowd didn't. They made War Emblem the 6-5 favorite and sent Sarava off at 70-1.

In the paddock, McPeek gave jockey Edgar Prado a leg up and said, "Go shock the world."

Jorgensen and Jenner made their way through the massive crowd and took a spot near the rail, at the end of the tunnel leading to the track. But Jorgensen was so nervous, she stepped back and stood several feet behind Jenner, next to one of the security officers. It was only eight months after 9/11 and security was extremely tight. War Emblem's owner, Prince Ahmed of Saudi Arabia, had decided to stay home. A year earlier his brother, Fahd Salman, had died mysteriously at age forty-six. (A month after the Belmont, Prince Ahmed would die of an apparent heart attack at age forty-three.)

Jenner's hopes were dashed one stride out of the gate when War Emblem stumbled badly, nearly going down, and got shuffled back in the field. There was no way the impetuous, front-running colt could win now. Gone was the Triple Crown; gone was the $5 million bonus that went along with it. Jenner could only watch in disgust. As he put it, "They're off; anyone want a hot dog?"

Sarava sat just off the pace most of the way, and when a small hole opened at the top of the stretch, Prado asked Sarava to go for it, and the colt charged through, just as Hayman had said he would.

Neither Jenner nor Jorgensen could see much. As the field turned for home, Jorgensen moved up next to

Jenner and kept jumping up and down, straining to see where Sarava was.

"Where's my horse?" she asked him.

With War Emblem backing up and out of contention, a disgusted Jenner told her, "Well, he's in front unless there are two freakin' Saravas in the race."

Once Jorgensen realized that it was Sarava on the lead, battling with Medaglia d'Oro, she started jumping up and down again.

At the wire, it was Sarava by a half-length. Jenner's disappointment soon turned to happiness for Jorgensen.

"Well, at least I won the Triple Crown by proxy," he said.

Afterward, he gave her a hug and a kiss and told her, "Well, now you can say you rode a Belmont winner, honey."

A year later Jorgensen was nearing her thirtieth birthday. In Norway, if a woman isn't married by thirty she is given a pepper mill as a mock gift and called a pepper maid. So, Jorgensen told Jenner, "You have two choices: You can either give me a pepper mill for my thirtieth birthday and have people make fun of me or you can give me a ring. It's your choice."

For her birthday, Jenner presented her with a pepper mill. No sooner had she said, "Darn it," when he gave her a ring and said, "Nobody's gonna make fun of you." Two years later they were married.

Sarava was taken away from Kenny McPeek later in

2002 and given to Baffert to train, but the colt never was able to regain his former glory and was retired to Cloverleaf Farms in Florida in 2004 after aggravating a suspensory injury that had plagued him.

In 2005, the same year Jorgensen and Jenner married, McPeek decided to retire from training, at least temporarily, to concentrate more on buying horses for his clients. He turned his horses over to Pitts, and Jorgensen, of course, went with her. The two have had a great deal of success together, sending out a number of classy stakes winners.

Jorgensen and Jenner have devised a schedule that allows them to be together the majority of the time, and one way to assure this was for Jenner to start exercising horses for her.

"Now I tell him what to do," Jorgensen said. "He's used to me barking orders anyway."

"It's not good for me," Jenner kidded. "I've never worked so hard in all my life. If she keeps it up, I'm gonna quit doing the laundry."

17

Smarty Mania
(2004)

Smarty Mania, a phenomenon that swept the nation from May to June 2004, was at its height.

It was a magical time for Thoroughbred racing. No horse in memory had affected people like Smarty Jones did. Perhaps it was his children's book name or where he came from or the courage he displayed after fracturing his skull and nearly losing his eye after a starting-gate accident as a two-year-old. He was so hideous looking when he arrived at the New Jersey Equine Clinic he was nicknamed Quasimodo.

To add to the intrigue, Smarty's owners, Roy and Pat Chapman, had hired trainer John Servis after their longtime trainer, Bob Camac, and his wife, Maryann, were murdered in December 2001 by Maryann's son.

The Chapmans had been devastated. With Roy already suffering from emphysema and requiring oxygen and a wheelchair to move about, they decided to sell most of their horses, keeping only two Pennsylvania-bred weanlings. One of them, a son of Elusive Quality, out of I'll Get Along, was born February 28, the same day as Pat Chapman's mother, whose nickname of Smarty Jones was passed on to the colt.

Smarty Jones built quite a following in Philadelphia, and when the undefeated colt won the Kentucky Derby, the City of Brotherly Love embraced him as it did its fictitious hero, Rocky. On the Saturday following the Derby, five thousand fans showed up at Philly Park just to watch him gallop, many of them children wearing Smarty Jones hats and T-shirts. On the Saturday after his resounding Preakness victory, nearly 10,000 fans jammed the apron and grandstand, many of them lined up outside the doors at 5:30 that morning. There was even talk of renaming Street Road, the main thoroughfare leading to the track, Smarty Jones Boulevard.

My most memorable experience covering Smarty Jones' Triple Crown actually began, of all places, at Citizens Bank Park, home of the Philadelphia Phillies.

Like many kids growing up playing Little League or sandlot baseball, I could only imagine what it would be like to stand on a big-league field in front of tens of thousands of fans and toss a ball around. So, needless to say, it was quite a thrill to be outside the Phillies' dugout at Citizens Bank Park having a catch, as we called it in Brooklyn, with Servis, who was about to throw out the first pitch before that night's game against the New

York Mets. I was there tagging along with *Daily Racing Form* photographer Mike Marten, who was shooting the ceremonies.

Servis had to limber up the old arm if he was going to zip one to the plate without embarrassing himself in front of the hometown fans. After being introduced to the players as they filed into the dugout from the clubhouse, Servis headed to the mound. "Now, ladies and gentlemen," the announcer bellowed into a microphone set up near home plate. "Please welcome the trainer of the athlete everyone is talking about: winner of the Kentucky Derby, winner of the Preakness, and gunning for the first Triple Crown since 1978 — Smarty Jones! Throwing out the first ball is Philly's own John Servis."

Driving through Philly after leaving the ballpark, I was amazed at how many signs and posters wishing Smarty good luck hung outside the Federal-and Georgian-style brick homes in Society Hill, one of the most pleasant and charming areas of Philadelphia.

The morning after the game Mike and I headed to the Philly Park backstretch in his rented SUV, having received special clearance to enter Smarty's sacred domain, where most were forbidden. Passing through the backstretch gate, it was as if we had in our possession the letters of transit from *Casablanca*.

The van that was to take Smarty to Belmont Park was already there, and at about 8:45 Smarty was led out of the barn, accompanied by Philly Park's head of security, Lance Morrell, and a pair of security officers. With one officer in front of the horse and the other behind, Smarty made his way to a small grassy paddock adjacent to the loading ramp. There he would wait like the rest of us for the Pennsylvania state troopers to arrive and escort him to the New Jersey state line, where he would then be escorted by New Jersey State Police up the Jersey Turnpike and over the George Washington Bridge. At that point, the New York police would take over the final leg of the trip.

Overhead, three TV helicopters hovered, waiting to record every step of Smarty's journey to the pantheon and the immortality that awaited him there.

Finally, two motorcycle troopers pulled up to the paddock fence. One of the troopers, Tim Henehan, thought he had seen it all. Six months earlier he had escorted President Bush. Now he was providing the same service for a horse.

"That was pretty special," he said, referring to the presidential escort. "But you've got a job to do, and you take it seriously no matter who you're escorting."

The other trooper, John Gladu, hopped off his motorcycle and immediately went through an odd transformation. He removed his helmet and sunglasses and put on a "Smarty Jones" hat. He then took out his camera and began taking pictures of Smarty in the paddock. "Hey, I'm just a fan," he said.

At 9:30, it was time for us to leave. I was driving Mike's SUV, with him riding shotgun to shoot the event. With Gladu and Henehan leading the way, the van, followed by several cars, pulled out of the backstretch and turned left on Galloway Road, where people were lined up, some giving a thumbs up as the van passed and shouting, "Go get 'em, Smarty."

As the van headed down the road, people stood in front of their homes with video cameras while others simply waved. The van then turned right on Street Road, the main thoroughfare in Bensalem, which had been blocked off to traffic. Cars were backed up for miles on Street Road, waiting for the "Philly Flyer" to make his way to the turnpike.

As soon as the van had turned on to Street Road, an unmarked police car and another motorcycle joined the procession. At the tollbooth to the turnpike, which was eerily devoid of cars, workers were out of their booths, applauding and shouting, "Go, Smarty." The whole scene was surrealistic. I followed as closely as possible, snatching my toll ticket and quickly regaining my place in line.

As the van headed east to New Jersey, people were gathered on the grass behind the service plaza taking pictures. I have no idea how they knew Smarty was coming and when he'd be passing by. Just past the service plaza, a billboard on the side of the turnpike read: "Look Out, New York. Smarty's Coming."

As I drove past the sign, I couldn't help but think of the many letters to the horse I had read a week earlier. One from ten-year-old Beach Cutler, of Jupiter, Florida, stood out. It read in part: "You have inspired me to run like a racehorse when I'm with my physical therapist and when I walk in the pool with my mom. My nurse times me when I'm pretending to race. You've lifted my spirits, and even though I'm on a ventilator, I feel as lucky as you. And please let your owner, Mr. Chapman, know that we are cheering for him to be in the best of health. I hope this letter gets to you, and that you know how much your incredible horse spirit has done for everyone."

And how do you describe the two Saturdays at Philadelphia Park when between five thousand and ten thousand fans showed up just to watch Smarty Jones gallop.

Here I was, smack in the middle of this fairy tale, tailing a horse van across three states and a hundred miles. By now, the unmarked police car had swung to the left of the van, preventing anyone from passing. Mike and I decided that when we came to the next toll, we'd simply follow the van through the booth, knowing that if we stopped to pay, we'd have a hell of a time catching up and getting back in the procession.

Just before the toll, with the Jersey police ready to take over, Gladu and Henehan made a U-turn and waved to the occupants peering out of the van. "OK, guys, good luck," Gladu shouted.

The heavily congested New Jersey Turnpike was an adventure, as I attempted to cling to what was left of our convoy. Occasionally, I'd catch a glimpse of *Philadelphia Daily News* writer Dick Jerardi also trying to maneuver his way back in line.

Mike and I had another decision to make: to continue running the tollbooths or not. We could fake it on the Jersey turnpike if we zipped through right behind the van, while flashing some phony credential. But the George Washington Bridge would be tricky. There weren't as many booths, and traffic would be much heavier.

"Hey, it's your rented car," I told Mike. "I'm just the driver."

Any traffic offenses from running toll booths would be in his name, not mine, and Mike needed to get to Belmont just before Smarty in order to get shots of him coming off the van. We decided to run the turnpike toll booth, making it through in good order, and we were looking good as the van got closer to the bridge and New York. After that it would be a piece of cake.

Mike and I were gloating over the success of our two-state pursuit when I noticed we were losing speed, although my foot was firmly pressed down on the accelerator. The vehicle was slowing down — and in the left lane of a six-lane highway.

The van began to fade from our view as we were now coasting about ten miles per hour. What the hell was happening? I looked at the fuel gauge, and, lo and behold, it was on empty. I couldn't believe it. We had run out of gas in the middle of who knows where, and I had to make my way across six lanes of traffic. With people shouting all kinds of obscenities, and more than a few middle fingers directed my way, I finally managed to get to the shoulder.

"How could you not fill up the tank?" I barked at Mike.

"How come you didn't look at the gauge?" he snapped back.

"Hell, it's not my car," I said. "I'm concentrating on driving, doing you a favor. You're supposed to make sure you have gas in the tank."

We quickly called a truce and concentrated on more important matters, such as getting gas. Fortunately, we were close to an entrance ramp. I was about to call AAA when Mike dashed out of the SUV and sprinted up the ramp, not having a clue where we were. All I knew was that we were somewhere near Fort Lee, New Jersey, maybe three or four miles from the "GW" bridge.

About ten or fifteen minutes later Mike returned in a pickup truck. The driver was a construction worker he had run into who just happened to have a can of gas on him. Mike paid him $100 for the gas and a ride back to the car.

"I wouldn't try making it all the way to Belmont Park," the guy told us after emptying the gas in our tank. "It'll be enough to get you to a gas station, but I wouldn't push my luck."

Mike still felt he could beat the van to Belmont, and nothing ever stood in Mike's way of getting a photograph. We knew the van wouldn't be allowed on the Cross Island Parkway and would have to go a different route. So, Mike said the hell with the guy's advice. He jumped behind the wheel and went into NASCAR mode, speeding across the Bronx, over the Whitestone Bridge, and on to the Cross

Island Parkway. The van would have to go out of its way and take the Clearview Expressway and then negotiate the busy streets.

Mike called one of his associates at Belmont, who told him the van hadn't arrived yet. He gunned the engine as the fuel gauge began easing its way back toward empty. We were getting closer and still no van. With Belmont in sight, Mike was told the van was just now pulling into the gate. It would still take several minutes for the driver to check in and then make his way through the backstretch to Barn 5, where Smarty would reside.

We zipped through the backstretch gate and headed toward Barn 5, defying every speed bump along the way. When we got to the barn, the van was there, but Smarty had not yet been unloaded. Mike jumped out, grabbed his camera, and dashed to the barn, arriving just as Smarty emerged from the van. I parked the car. Mike got his shot. We looked at each other and laughed. Piece of cake.

18

Alex, We Hardly Knew Ya
(2005)

It was sweltering at Belmont for an early morning in June. The temperatures were climbing quickly toward ninety degrees, and even the railbirds' clothes clung like wetsuits in the high humidity.

Afleet Alex, as was his custom, had already been out for his early morning 1½-mile jog and was due back to the track at 8:30 for a strong gallop in preparation for the 2005 Belmont Stakes. Alex had thrust himself into the national spotlight with a remarkable, death-defying victory in the Preakness, following a third-place finish in the Kentucky Derby. A victory in the Belmont would escalate him to the cult-hero status accorded his immediate predecessors Smarty Jones and Funny Cide, both of whom had won the Kentucky Derby and Preakness, only to fall short in the 1½-mile Belmont.

Accompanied by trainer Tim Ritchey on his pony, Alex stepped onto the track and proceeded to turn in a strong

1½-mile gallop. Trainer Bobby Frankel and I watched him from the trainer's stand, located by the clubhouse turn.

"Boy, he looks good," said Frankel, who was becoming more of an Afleet Alex fan each day. He was amazed at what the colt had accomplished all year with a twice-a-day training regimen. It was unheard of for a horse to go to the track two times a day, and many had been second-guessing Ritchey's methods, including Frankel. A former event rider, Ritchey was a big believer in building up a horse's stamina. Not many Thoroughbreds could stand up to such a regimen, but Ritchey thought Afleet Alex was one of those rare individuals who not only could handle it but also would thrive on it.

Undoubtedly, Frankel was impressed with the gallop he had just seen. A few minutes later we both started down the steps from the trainer's stand. At one point I looked back at the track and couldn't believe what I was seeing. Afleet Alex was galloping by again, this time at an even quicker clip. I couldn't recall a horse ever galloping twice around Belmont's 1½-mile oval. This was a three-mile gallop in stifling heat, and he was actually getting stronger as he went along.

Frankel could only shake his head. When Alex and Ritchey came off the track, the horse's body — from neck to hind end — looked like a road map, each vein seemingly on the outside of his frame. Ritchey, his shirt soaked with sweat, looked down and broke into a smile. "Do you think he's fit?" he asked.

The more Frankel thought about it, the more convinced he was that this horse was something special.

"You know what?" he said at his barn one morning, as if experiencing some revelation. "I was thinking, Afleet Alex just may be that good. Maybe he is a Seattle Slew or an Affirmed or one of those kinds. Looking at how fast he's run on his [speed] Sheet numbers, the fact that he's still around and doing what he's doing is pretty amazing."

The Cinderella story of Afleet Alex can only be told here in condensed form, as its many story lines intertwine. His dam, Maggy Hawk, a daughter of Hawkster, was unable to produce milk and could not provide her foal with colostrum, the antibody-rich fluid that helps prevent disease in newborns. Because a foal has only a 10 percent chance of surviving without colostrum, a nurse mare had to be found for the son of Northern Afleet. During the twelve days it took to obtain one, breeder John Silvertand's nine-year-old daughter, Lauren, fed the foal milk every day out of a Coors Lite bottle. A photo of Lauren feeding Alex eventually made its way onto the colt's Web site and into other publications.

Afleet Alex was considered an ugly duckling growing up, and John Devers, who had acquired the colt in a coin toss from Silvertand (the two men had owned Maggie Hawk and a few other mares in partnership and had flipped a coin to get first choice of the weanlings), decided to sell him privately to Joseph Allen for $150,000. After the colt was broken and put in training at Robert

Scanlon's training center in Williston, Florida, the same advisers who told Allen to buy him recommended he get rid of him. So, Allen consigned him to the Fasig-Tipton Timonium two-year-old sale, where he was purchased by Ritchey for his new client, Cash is King Stable, for $75,000. Headed by managing partner Chuck Zacney, Cash is King is made up of a group of small-time owners from the Philadelphia area. Afleet Alex was their first horse.

Afleet Alex was an instant success, winning his career debut at Delaware Park in spectacular fashion by more than eleven lengths. It was a performance that didn't go unnoticed by trainer Nick Zito, who was running a horse in the following race.

Zito's assistant, Tim Poole, had arrived just before the race. After stopping at the receiving barn, he had driven to the horsemen's parking lot on the clubhouse turn. As Poole got out of his car, the horses from the previous race were pulling up on the turn. Just then, his phone rang. It was Zito, his voice bursting with excitement.

"Did you see that?" he bellowed.

"See what?" Poole asked, not knowing what he was talking about.

"That race. Did you see it?" Zito said.

Poole, not knowing where this race had taken place, asked Zito what track he was referring to.

"Right there where you are," said Zito. "Get a hold of Ritchey and tell him, 'Whatever you want for that horse just name your price.'"

But Cash is King wouldn't sell.

Alex went on to win an allowance race by twelve lengths before winning the Sanford Stakes and Hopeful Stakes, both at Saratoga.

During Alex's two-year-old campaign, which also saw him finish second in the Champagne Stakes and Breeders' Cup Juvenile, Zacney, who had named the colt after his son, Alex, heard about Alex Scott, a young girl diagnosed with neuroblastoma, an aggressive form of childhood cancer. Alex Scott had decided to open a lemonade stand in her front yard to raise money for cancer research. Word spread around the globe, and Alex's Lemonade Stands began popping up all over, earning millions of dollars in donations.

When Zacney first learned of Alex's Lemonade Stand, he naturally thought of Afleet Alex, his son, and two of the other partners' children, Alex and Alexandra. In August 2004, Alex Scott lost her battle with cancer at age eight, but her lemonade stands would live on. In late September 2004, after Afleet Alex had won his fourth straight race, Zacney pledged $5,000 to the fund and donated a portion of Afleet Alex's future winnings.

As Afleet Alex's fame grew, so did the story of Lauren feeding the young colt through a beer bottle. Before the Kentucky Derby, Silvertand and his wife, Carolyn, were contacted by Nevada Governor Kenny Guinn and first lady Dema Guinn, who said they were starting a cancer fund campaign and wanted to use the Silvertands' photo of Lauren and Afleet Alex to help bolster it.

Alex Scott was not the only one with cancer associated with Afleet Alex. In October 2002, Silvertand had been diagnosed with terminal cancer and given only a couple of months to live. More than two years after the original diagnosis, Afleet Alex was still working his life-prolonging magic on his breeder. As Afleet Alex's career progressed, Silvertand decided to discontinue chemotherapy and leave it "in God's hands" in order to enjoy and participate in Afleet Alex's career.

After winning the Arkansas Derby in a romp, Afleet Alex arrived at Churchill Downs for the Kentucky Derby. The one-time ugly duckling had veteran horsemen scratching their proverbial heads, unable to comprehend how this still uninspiring-looking little horse could be such a swan on the racetrack and accomplish the things he had throughout his two-year-old and early three-year-old campaigns

One morning, shortly after arriving at Churchill Downs some two weeks before the Derby, Alex was walking off the track and passed D. Wayne Lukas' barn. Lukas, standing outside the barn, took one look at the horse and commented, "That little muskrat is Afleet Alex?"

Alex may have looked like a little muskrat off the track, but on the track he was sheer poetry, with a smooth, efficient stride and an explosive turn of foot.

In the Kentucky Derby, Alex put in a big run but had to settle for third, beaten one length by 50-1 shot Giacomo, with 71-1 shot Closing Argument second.

What no one knew, however, was that Alex had

come out of the Derby with a lung infection that the veterinarian said was a three on a scale of one to five.

Ritchey and the Cash is King partners never said a word about it at the time because Alex also had suffered a bad lung infection while finishing sixth in the Rebel Stakes in March, and the last thing they wanted to do was use that same excuse again.

So, it was on to the Preakness. Silvertand, meanwhile, continued to defy the doctors' prognostications and traveled to Baltimore from his home in Lake Worth, Florida, by himself the day before the Preakness. Although he had been feeling ill and was seriously thinking about staying home, he decided he had to be there for the race. This is what he had stayed alive to witness.

"Whatever happens, I didn't expect to be here this long, so it's all been wonderful for me," he said after witnessing Alex's unforgettable win in the Preakness. "I try to plan things around Alex to keep me going. Right now, I'm planning on being at the Belmont, then the Travers in beautiful Saratoga, and the Breeders' Cup. I can see it all in my mind. I don't notice my pain because of all the excitement that's going on. Maybe when everything quiets down tonight I won't feel as good as everyone else, but I'm still going to feel pretty good.

"This has been so much more than just a horse story. You have Alex's Lemonade Stand, which has been benefiting from all the publicity, and has gotten a great many people interested in horse racing. There are so many wonderful things in this world we will never get to see, and I'm just so glad to be here."

If America wasn't familiar with the Afleet Alex story before the Preakness, it was afterward. Almost every TV sports and news program and major newspaper showed footage or photos of Afleet Alex's recovery from a near-disastrous fall, considered by everyone who saw it one of the most courageous and athletic feats ever witnessed on a racetrack or any other sports arena for that matter.

Although it was an unscripted scene that took only a heartbeat to play out, the images will remain frozen in time. One second, Afleet Alex is flying past his opponents as if moving in fast forward, and the next he is virtually picking himself up off the ground.

Afleet Alex had clipped the heels of the erratic-running Scrappy T at the top of the stretch, stumbling so badly his nose was inches off the ground. With his front legs spread-eagled, and jockey Jeremy Rose grabbing on to the colt's mane for dear life, Afleet Alex somehow was able to stay on his feet. Most horses would never have recovered, and those that did would have taken awhile to regain their composure. But Afleet Alex proved on that day what all those around him already knew: He was not like other horses.

He picked himself up, changed leads in a matter of two strides, and charged past Scrappy T. He then drew off to win by 4¾ lengths, while still turning in one of the fastest final three-sixteenths in Preakness history.

Nick Zito, who wound up running five horses in the

Kentucky Derby that year, still felt a closeness to Afleet Alex and was amazed at what he overcame.

"I've been on the racetrack since I was a kid, and I have never seen anything like what he did in the Preakness. And I mean never," he said. "His whole story, with Alex's Lemonade Stand, is so inspiring. After the Kentucky Derby, when I got beat with all five of my horses, all I thought about was Alex Scott, and that put everything in its proper perspective."

Following the Preakness, Alex came back three weeks later and demolished his opposition in the Belmont Stakes, winning by seven lengths. One of the most everlasting images of Afleet Alex was after he had won the "Test of the Champion."

As Ritchey walked back to the barn following the post-race interviews, he was more reflective about the gift he and the Cash is King partners had been given.

"I've never even dreamt of a horse like this," he said. "He's an absolutely amazing animal. I may get some good horses in the years to come, but I'll never have another one like him; no way, shape, or form. He's just a special, special horse, and now everyone is seeing it for themselves."

Afleet Alex apparently did everything fast, as he surprisingly had already left the test barn when Ritchey went to check in on him. Back at his barn, Ritchey, along with J.J. Graci and Anita Saint Clair, who handled all of Afleet Alex's marketing and merchandise, toasted Alex's victory with champagne.

The three, along with Zacney and his wife, Carol, recently had visited New York Presbyterian Hospital, bringing Afleet Alex posters, caps, shirts, and buttons to the children and telling them of the horse "who almost fell, but didn't let it stop him, and how he kept fighting just like you guys are doing."

In the quiet of the evening hour, all was finally tranquil as Afleet Alex grazed contentedly while Ritchey looked on, holding his jacket under his arm and wiping the sweat off his forehead. As if feeling the urge to be close to the horse, he walked over and took the shank and immediately gave Alex several firm pats on the neck before running his hand over the colt's back and hindquarters.

Alex returned to grazing until he was interrupted by a sound off in the distance. It was the faint call of the day's final race. A wide-eyed Alex turned his head toward the grandstand and then turned his body until he was facing it. He picked his head up and cocked his ears and did not move a muscle until the call was over.

"He's probably saying, 'Heck, I can whip them, too,'" Ritchey said. As soon as the race ended, Alex calmly walked back into his stall. Rose showed up later and spent a few special moments with the colt. Then the light was shut off. All was dark, except for the glow emanating from the stall. It was the same glow that had reached out and touched so many people across the country. On this day it had reached out and touched tens of thousands of appreciative fans at Belmont Park who, after several recent years of disappointment, finally went home happy.

Sadly, that was to be the last racing fans would ever see of Afleet Alex. In July a small hairline fracture was discovered in his ankle. Surgery performed at the New Jersey Equine Clinic appeared to be successful, and Alex was put back in training in early September. No one could have imagined that in only sixty-five days, Alex would go from having surgery to repair a fracture to working five furlongs at Belmont Park in :59⅘, the fastest work on the tab.

But in late November, a new problem appeared on a set of xeroradiographs in the form of an abnormal wedge-shaped section of bone abutting the original fracture line. Veterinarian Patricia Hogan said she believed the "terrible jar" the colt experienced in the Preakness was the root of this problem, as well as the original fracture. With this latest injury only likely to worsen with training, the decision was made to retire the horse.

Alex's Lemonade Stands continued to pop up across the country, showing up in supermarkets and other establishments. Her stands had collected about $11,000 at the Kentucky Derby and $17,000 at the Preakness. On Belmont Stakes Day, more than one thousand lemonade stands were in business, many of them at racetracks and wagering facilities across the country. By the end of 2005, more than $3.5 million dollars had been raised, a large portion due to the media attention raised by a small, non-descript champion named Afleet Alex.

All of Afleet Alex's merchandising material was emblazoned with a lemon, signifying the stable's support of the fund. A portion of the merchandising proceeds also was donated to Alex's Lemonade Stand.

John Silvertand stayed alive long enough to experience all the thrills Alex provided on the racetrack, but, he, like little Alex Scott, lost his battle with cancer.

19

The Day That Shook the Racing World
(2006)

A light May rain dampened the lush green expanse of the Fair Hill Training Center, located approximately sixty miles from Pimlico Race Course. The 2006 Preakness Stakes was five days away, and Kentucky Derby winner Barbaro was beginning to pick up his training, galloping strongly over the seven-furlong wood-chip track.

With the chaotic atmosphere of the Derby behind them, Barbaro and trainer Michael Matz were enjoying their final days of tranquility in this pastoral setting before facing the pandemonium of the Preakness. Far removed from Pimlico, or any other racetrack, Matz' barn is nestled on the fringes of dense woodlands and bordered on the opposite side by gently rolling hills and open spaces, creating an idyllic atmosphere. The winding horse path, which rises and dips ever so slightly, first passes Matz' two paddocks and eight round pens and then stretches over the horizon to the dirt and wood-chip tracks.

Barbaro, only ten days earlier, had been surrounded by hordes of photographers and cameramen as he made his way to the Churchill Downs winner's circle. Now, here he was, with Matz aboard the pony, ambling along, an occasional swallow darting across his path.

Following his spectacular six-length romp in the Derby, many people already were conceding Barbaro the Triple Crown. With his tactical speed, sweeping stride, and stamina-laden pedigree, he seemed to have the 1½-mile Belmont Stakes at his mercy. Only the Preakness stood between him and immortality.

Normally, by Wednesday of Preakness week, the Pimlico stakes barn is a hotbed of activity. Most of the horses competing in the second jewel of the Triple Crown are already on the grounds, and members of the media are beating a path in and out of the hospitality room, coffee and doughnuts in hand.

This year not a soul stirred in the stakes barn. On Wednesday morning the only occupant was Oreo, a nineteen-year-old Paint horse recruited as a pony for Santa Anita Derby winner Brother Derek, who had finished a troubled fourth in the Kentucky Derby.

For four consecutive mornings I drove from Baltimore to Fair Hill to watch Barbaro train and to soak up the beauty of the Maryland countryside. Each morning the number of media increased as reporters and photographers carpooled from their respective hotels, some nearby.

Matz, for the most part, was intolerant of the media, especially those who asked questions he considered inane or irrelevant. For months leading up to the Derby, he had listened and read how his conservative approach to the race was not the right way to get a horse to the first Saturday in May. It seemed as if his every move was being questioned.

Following Wednesday evening's post-position draw at the ESPN Zone in the Inner Harbor, Matz decided to have dinner with his wife, DD, and Barbaro's owners, Roy and Gretchen Jackson, before addressing the media, most of whom were on deadline. It was quite a sight, as a cluster of reporters hovered over Matz' booth, waiting for him to finish eating. The following morning he remained at Fair Hill instead of attending the traditional Alibi Breakfast at Pimlico, a decision that did not sit well with track officials.

But if Matz knew you and trusted you, he could be extremely charming. His smile is infectious, as is his soft-spoken demeanor.

On Thursday morning, while walking through Matz' barn, I noticed a small "w" next to Barbaro's name on the activity sheet. At first I thought it meant "walk" but soon discovered from a barn worker it stood for "work."

Barbaro galloped around the dirt track under regular exercise rider Peter Brette, who then let the colt open up in the final two furlongs. I clocked his quarter-mile work in :24 seconds. It was Barbaro's only work between the

Derby and Preakness. The following morning he was off to Pimlico.

Barbaro arrived at "Old Hilltop" by van to a hero's welcome as a gauntlet of photographers, cameramen, and writers greeted racing's newest superstar. Barbaro stared out the van window at the throng that had gathered. The scene was a stark contrast to the halcyon days of the past two weeks.

The following day Barbaro was once again on a van staring out the window, this time on his way to the New Bolton Medical Center in Kennett Square, Pennsylvania. There Dr. Dean Richardson would perform a four-hour surgical procedure in an attempt to save the colt, who had broken down shortly after the start of the Preakness in front of a stunned crowd.

As the van departed Pimlico with a police escort for the nearly two-hour drive to New Bolton, people wandered about in shock, some still showing the signs of recently shed tears. They lined the streets to bid him farewell; many believed for the last time.

Triumph and tragedy are elemental in Thoroughbred racing. The horrific injury suffered by Barbaro in the Preakness highlights the inherent tragedy of the sport. The triumph was Bernardini's spectacular victory, one that deserved to be played out in front of cheering, appreciative fans instead of a grief-stricken crowd jolted into stunned silence. These two faces of racing formed one conflicting picture as Bernardini, 5¼ lengths ahead of his closest pursuer, charged past Barbaro, who stood helplessly just past the finish line in front of a record 118,402 fans who had come to see greatness.

Just seconds before, Barbaro had been running, a cool May breeze in his face and adrenaline pumping through his body. All was as it should have been. Then came a sensation he had never felt before. His right hind leg, which had helped propel him to victory after victory, suddenly became lifeless, shattered by three fractures that crushed his pastern into twenty fragments of bone.

I had been watching the race with *Sports Illustrated*'s Tim Laydon on the jumbo screen from the inside the rail. Simultaneously, we both asked each other, "Where's Barbaro?" We both then turned around and saw him behind us. It was apparent he had broken down and was in distress.

The cheers that had been reserved for Barbaro on this day were replaced by shrieks and pleas not to euthanize the horse, which seemed a possibility after a screen was placed in front of the colt, shielding him from the crowd.

"No! No! No!" one woman by the rail screeched in utter despair at the sight of the screen being put up. "Do not put that horse down! Don't you dare put him down. I'll buy him for a dollar."

Shouts of "take him home" and "get him on the van" also were heard from the frantic fans who were witness to the gut-wrenching images directly in front of them. Many wept uncontrollably as track veterinarians attended the once-mighty Barbaro, placing a Kimzey splint on the right hind leg.

After what seemed an eternity the screen was removed, and Matz helped open the door of the ambulance. As Barbaro was led on, a round of applause erupted from the stands.

Darrell Haire of the Jockeys' Guild had rushed onto the track to console a distraught Edgar Prado, Barbaro's jockey, who was bent over in anguish.

Roy and Gretchen Jackson headed back to the barn to see their horse.

"You don't expect something like this," Gretchen said. "Being beaten, yes, but not this. If you followed this horse, you had to love him."

That was all she had to say.

"Excuse me," she said almost apologetically. "I have some phone calls I need to make because I have a family that's waiting to figure out what to do."

As the large gathering of media searched for information, a solitary figure leaned against a fence by the loading ramp, staring off into space. Matz' daughter, Michelle, who works as an exercise rider for her father and whom I had gotten to know during my mornings at Fair Hill, had just a short while earlier been brimming with confidence that Barbaro would put on a show similar to the one in the Kentucky Derby two weeks before.

"He was a great horse anyway," she said.

When I asked her why she used the past tense, she

shook her head slightly and replied, "It's not good. They're going to try to save him, but I don't know. This horse has always been such a professional. When he walked out of the barn today, I looked at him and I knew he was going to kick butt. Peter told me, 'He's unbeatable, Michelle.' It's so hard because he loves to run."

Just then, Michelle saw Prado heading toward the barn and ran after him. The two hugged, burying their heads in each other's shoulders.

"I'm sorry," Prado said.

"It's not your fault," she replied.

A noticeably shaken DD Matz walked to her car and stopped briefly to provide information.

"He's handling it like the true champion he is," she said. "He's going to the best place possible, with the best surgeons, so he'll get the best care he can."

Her emotions then caught up with her and she was unable to continue.

"I really don't want to talk about this," she said. "I'm not going to discuss it. I'm sorry."

I couldn't help but think back to the tremendous air of anticipation earlier that morning. Brother Derek was getting some support after his horrendous trip in the Kentucky Derby, and both he and Barbaro went out to the track at 5:45 a.m. for one final gallop. The track was only open from 5:30 to 6:00 and for Preakness horses only.

As Barbaro and Matz left the barn, Brother Derek's trainer, Dan Hendricks, said to Matz, "Let's get out there and get it over with this morning," to which Matz responded with a smile, "It's going to happen soon enough, Dan."

As the horses were called to the paddock for the Preakness, Matz and Hendricks, who had developed a tremendous respect for each other over the past three weeks, wished each other luck. I'll never forget Hendricks' final words to Matz: "Safe trip."

A short while later it would be Bernardini who stormed to victory. Sadly, when the winner returned from the detention barn after the race, neither the fans nor the media paid any attention.

Barbaro, who had been sedated and placed in a four-layer padded bandage, arrived at New Bolton just after nine o'clock. Outside the gates of New Bolton a large crowd had gathered, with many people holding signs and placards wishing the colt well. Some were in tears as the van passed through the entrance. Local TV stations had helicopters overhead filming Barbaro's arrival, just as they had done with 2004 Derby winner Smarty Jones on the much happier occasion of his triumphant return to Philadelphia Park.

As darkness fell on Pimlico, Bernardini's jockey, Javier Castellano, showed up at the barn and went right over to his colt, who had been posing for pictures with several visitors. "I told you," he said to the horse. "I came to see you last night, and I gave you a kiss and told you we were going to win."

About thirty yards away, at the darkened end of the

barn, Barbaro's hotwalker, Ricardo Orozco, prepared to return to Fair Hill along with groom Eduardo Hernandez. It would be a long ride home. The equipment was packed, and soon all evidence that Barbaro had been there would be gone.

Stall 40, which traditionally is home to the Kentucky Derby winner, is empty at least forty-five to fifty weeks out of the year. But never this empty.

....

Early Days

20

Belmont Buddies

In 1968 and 1969, runners with ties to venerable racing stables thwarted back-to-back Triple Crown bids. Had Calumet Farm's Forward Pass won the 1968 Belmont Stakes, it would have tainted the Triple Crown for all time. The colt had been placed first in the Kentucky Derby following the controversial disqualification of Dancer's Image due to a positive test for the drug butazolidan. Forward Pass went on to romp in the Preakness, putting himself in line to become the first Triple Crown winner in twenty years.

Forward Pass ran a winning race in the Belmont, but an exciting newcomer named Stage Door Johnny, owned by Greentree Stable, swept past him in the final sixteenth to win by 1½ lengths, saving the sport the ignominy of having to put an asterisk next to a Triple Crown winner. Stage Door Johnny, a flashy, blaze-faced chestnut, proved the Belmont win was no fluke when he went on to score impressive victories in the Saranac and Dwyer handicaps, the latter under 129 pounds. An injury ended his career following the Dwyer, and he retired to Greentree Stud, where he passed on his stamina for generations.

In 1969 Majestic Prince, who had been the most expensive yearling ever sold at auction, attempted to become the first undefeated Triple Crown winner in history after two narrow victories over Rokeby Stable's plucky little Arts and Letters. Many thought Majestic Prince should have been disqualified for shutting off Arts and Letters in the Preakness, especially as he had only beaten his rival by a head. Majestic Prince's trainer, Johnny Longden, was not happy with the way the colt came out of the Preakness and contemplated passing the Belmont but owner Frank McMahon overruled him.

Arts and Letters, a son of Ribot, was bred to run all day, and when he came back after the Preakness and easily defeated older horses in the Metropolitan Handicap, many rightly predicted he would turn the tables on Majestic Prince in the Belmont. The race was no contest, as Arts and Letters drew off to a five-length victory over Majestic Prince. He went undefeated the rest of the year, easily winning the Jim Dandy, Travers, Woodward, and Jockey Club Gold Cup by an average margin of more than eight lengths to nail down Horse of the Year honors. Following his retirement in 1970, due to an injury, he joined Stage Door Johnny at Greentree Stud.

Arts and Letters was placed in the paddock next to Stage Door Johnny, and the two immediately hit it off. They would remain buddies and neighbors until Stage Door Johnny's death in 1996 at age thirty-one. When Stage Door Johnny died, Arts and Letters replaced him as the oldest living Belmont Stakes winner.

As soon as Arts and Letters arrived at Greentree, the two would race each other constantly. They would start at the top of the hill and race full speed along the fence, stepping on the brakes just before reaching the paddock gate, where they would kick up a cloud of dust. They would then glance over to each other, as if looking to see who had won, and then walk slowly back up the hill and come charging back down.

The two stallions became so close that when adjacent Gainesway Farm took over the Greentree property in 1989, part of the agreement was that the two Belmont winners remain together.

During their active years as stallions, whenever Stage Door Johnny would go to the breeding shed, Arts and Letters would get upset and start running around his paddock. And Stage Door Johnny would do the same whenever Arts and Letters went to the breeding shed.

They continued to race each other for years until they got too old. In their later years they would stand under the same shade tree that separated their paddocks and just keep each other company.

To get an idea how long they were together, James Kennon, whose father worked with the broodmares at

Greentree, began helping out around the farm in 1963 at the age of nine and then started working with Stage Door Johnny and Arts and Letters when he was sixteen. At the time of Stage Door Johnny's death, he was forty-three and still working with the two horses.

Both stallions left their mark on the Triple Crown. Arts and Letters sired 1980 Preakness winner Codex, and Stage Door Johnny was the broodmare sire of 1994 Kentucky Derby winner Go for Gin.

Following Stage Door Johnny's death, Arts and Letters stayed out in the paddock twenty-four hours a day, being checked and fed twice a day. He remained in good spirits and relatively good health, but in 1998, at the age of thirty-two, the infirmities of old age caught up to him. He was buried next to his longtime friend. The two oldest living Belmont winners were gone.

21

A Warhorse
Named Jim French
(1970)

The story of Jim French, one of the most indestructible, indefatigable horses of the modern era, has faded into history, taking with it the colt's remarkable feats of durability on the racetrack and the notorious final chapter of his career, in which the Travers favorite was impounded by the Saratoga County sheriff's office and not permitted to run.

But it was the Triple Crown and the road leading there that earned Jim French the title of Iron Horse. Actually, that is too mundane a term. There is no title one can give Jim French because no other horse has had to endure the schedule he did. And by running race after race, week after week, he has earned a special place in Triple Crown history, even though he did not win a Triple Crown race.

Jim French was a smallish brown colt who brought

his trainer, John Campo, into the national spotlight. But Campo's training of Jim French would have brought criticism and hostility from today's Internet racing fans, who are much more animal-rights conscious than the racing fans of the early seventies. Not only did the son of Graustark stand up to Campo's unprecedented schedule, he actually seemed to thrive on it. Regardless of the distance, whether six furlongs or 1½ miles, Jim French never failed to hit the board during his Triple Crown campaign.

Campo, who would go on to become one of the top trainers in the country, later would say when asked why he ran Jim French so often, "I didn't know any better then. I had only been training for a few years, and if I had known better I wouldn't have run him so many times. He wasn't a big horse, and small horses do hold up better than big horses."

Hold up is an understatement. As excessive as Campo's methods were, his ability to keep Jim French in top racing condition for so long actually was a remarkable achievement. By the time Jim French arrived in Florida in December 1970 to begin preparing for the Triple Crown races, he had already crammed eleven races into five months, racing four times in November alone, including a victory in the Remsen Stakes.

• On December 26 he engaged in a thrilling stretch duel with Sir Dagonet to win the 1¹⁄₁₆-mile Miami Beach Handicap at Tropical Park.

• Two weeks later he just got up to win the 1¹⁄₁₆-mile

Dade Metropolitan Handicap at Tropical by a nose, carrying top weight of 125 pounds and conceding ten pounds to the runner-up.

• Eleven days later, this time at Hialeah, he dropped back to six furlongs and finished a fast-closing fourth in the Hibiscus Stakes, beaten only 1¼ lengths by the brilliant Executioner.

• He was back two weeks later, coming from tenth at the top of the stretch to win the seven-furlong Bahamas Stakes by a head, with the regally bred His Majesty third.

• Two weeks later he was beaten a head by His Majesty in the 1⅛-mile Everglades Stakes but was disqualified to fifth for bearing in down the stretch.

• Like clockwork he was back in the gate two weeks later, coming from nineteen lengths back to finish third behind Executioner in the 1⅛-mile Flamingo Stakes.

• Instead of waiting for the Florida Derby, not only did Jim French run seventeen days later but he shipped up to New York, where he finished third to the early Kentucky Derby favorite Hoist the Flag in the seven-furlong Bay Shore Stakes, run in a scorching 1:21.

• Back in Florida a week later, he closed fast to finish third to Eastern Fleet in the Florida Derby, run in 1:47⅖, just three-fifths off the stakes record.

• Not content to wait for one final Derby prep, Campo put Jim French on a plane to California and ran him one week later in the Santa Anita Derby, which he won by 1¾ lengths in 1:48⅕.

• Two weeks later the colt was back in New York, where he finished a solid fourth to stablemate Good Behaving in the Wood Memorial.

So, Jim French entered the grueling Triple Crown series, having competed in ten stakes at five different racetracks in a little more than four months, traveling from New York to Florida to New York to Florida to California and back to New York. Although most horses would have been totally wiped out, Jim French went on to finish a fast-closing second to Canonero II in the Kentucky Derby, third in Canonero's track record-breaking Preakness, and a fast-closing second in the Belmont Stakes, in which he made up more than five lengths in the final furlong, falling three-quarters of a length short of catching the victorious Pass Catcher.

Instead of being given a well-earned vacation following arguably the most ambitious Triple Crown campaign ever, Jim French amazingly was back in the starting gate two weeks after the Belmont, finishing fourth in the one-mile Pontiac Grand Prix (formerly the Arlington Classic) at Arlington Park. Following his first three-week "vacation" since the previous November, he shipped to California, where he finished second in the 1 1/4-mile Hollywood Derby, giving the winner, Bold Reason, thirteen pounds. One week later he was back in New York, winning the 1 1/4-mile Dwyer Handicap, conceding from twelve to fifteen pounds to the rest of the field.

In less than eight months Jim French had run in sixteen stakes from six furlongs to 1 1/2 miles, never finishing worse than fourth (except for his disqualification). During that time he competed at ten different racetracks, made two round-trip cross-country flights at a time when Eastern horses rarely flew to California, and logged almost 20,000 miles of traveling.

Jim French resurfaced four weeks after the Dwyer and ran an uncharacteristic ninth as the 2-1 favorite in the Monmouth Invitational Handicap. After the race it was discovered that a spur in the colt's right knee had broken off. Several people around the horse, however, were convinced he had been "gotten to."

When Campo sent Jim French to Saratoga for the Travers, all hell broke loose. Prior to the race it was announced that the Saratoga County sheriff's office had impounded Jim French. The stewards refused his entry for the Travers. State steward Francis P. Dunne called it "the most complex racing situation I've ever encountered."

A hidden ownership issue surrounding the horse had been discovered through a loan taken out by Jim French's co-owner Frank Caldwell, who had purchased him from Ralph Wilson, the breeder, during the colt's two-year-old campaign.

Caldwell, a Long Island furniture executive, had sold 70 percent of Jim French to one Etta Sarant and then had taken out a loan from the Citizens National Bank and Trust Company of Lexington, Kentucky, receiving a $130,000 advance after stating on his affidavit he solely owned Jim French. Leslie Combs II, a director of the bank, assured that Jim French would stand at his Spendthrift Farm in Lexington.

However, Mrs. Sarant, in whose name Jim French raced in the Monmouth Invitational, had neither an owner's license in New York nor an interest in applying for one. After the Monmouth Invitational, Jim French was resold to construction executive Fred Cole, but he, too, had been suspended by the New York Racing Commission for failure to appear to give testimony in the case. That left Jim French without an owner.

Dunne said at the time, "We have a real can of worms on our hands."

He was right. Officers of the Saratoga County sheriff's office then filed a writ of attachment on behalf of Citizens Bank. The New York Racing Commission, sensing a possible cover-up, began investigating the ownership of Jim French and several other horses supposedly owned by Caldwell.

According to the commission's findings, the true owner or part-owner of Jim French and the other horses was R. Robert LiButti doing business as Robert Presti. LiButti was a New Jersey gambler and racehorse consultant who bought and sold horses for years. The commission also concluded that the horse's ownership had been concealed from racing authorities and stated that LiButti had been barred from racing in 1968 due to alleged ties to organized crime. He denied any involvement and maintained it was a misunderstanding and that he had been exonerated of any wrongdoing.

LiButti, who also went by the name Nicholas Spadea at times, said that undisclosed ownership was common in racing, and his ownership of Jim French was not done to defraud the public, claiming that no crime had been committed. For years after the Jim French incident, he denied all charges and claimed to be a victim of a conspiracy to ban him from the sport.

On October 13, 1971, the New York Racing Commission suspended Campo, Ralph Wilson, and trainer George Poole for thirty days for their roles in the concealed ownership. Caldwell was ordered to appear before the commission to "show cause why his license should not be revoked."

Jim French was not allowed to run in the Travers. Because of the complexity of the case, and the danger of his knee eventually splitting due to the spur that had broken off, he was retired and sold (it was never officially reported by whom) to art dealer Daniel Wildenstein for $1 million and retired to Haras de la Verrerie in France, where he sired only six stakes winners. He was then sent to Japan in 1977. His name did show up in America as the broodmare sire of Breeders' Cup Mile winner and grass champion Steinlen.

Jim French has long since disappeared. Shamefully, the vast majority of today's racing fans have never even heard of him. He was a true Thoroughbred in every sense of the word. He gave 100 percent every time, despite being subjected to one of the most grueling racing schedules of any horse in the history of the sport.

Afterword

....

Quotes, Quips, and Quickies

The following are some of the more memorable quotes I have either been given or overheard during the Triple Crown trail throughout the years.

• Johnny Campo delivered the best post-race quote following Pleasant Colony's victory in the 1981 Kentucky Derby. But first the stage has to be set. This was pre-Nick Zito, who had been Campo's assistant years earlier. The Kentucky bluebloods had never been exposed to a New York trainer like Campo. So, you can imagine their reaction when ABC commentator Jim McKay reminded Campo on national TV that the trainer had predicted Pleasant Colony would win the Derby.

The not-so-humble Campo's response: "I'm a good horse trainer, pal. Don't you forget it."

• Talk about ruffling feathers: How about owner Robert Lehmann saying after Dust Commander's victory in the

1970 Kentucky Derby that winning the Derby wasn't as big a thrill for him as bagging big game in Africa. Yikes!

• Bob Baffert watching favored Cavonnier's run fizzle out at the top of the stretch in the Preakness: "Houston, we have a problem."

• Speaking of Baffert, a few days before the 1997 Kentucky Derby, I accompanied him to a hair salon on Frankfort Avenue prior to going to dinner. As a new customer, he was asked to fill out a brief questionnaire. Under profession, Baffert wrote, "porn star." The expression on the female hair stylist's face after reading it was priceless.

• Credit Wayne Lukas for the most cocksure prediction prior to a Triple Crown race. As he prepared Editor's Note to be schooled in the paddock the day before the 1996 Belmont Stakes, Lukas said in a slow and succinct manner, "I'm going to say this — you are looking at the winner right now. I know every guy in the business has said that to you, but they won't beat this horse tomorrow — rain or shine and despite the jockey change [to the little-used Rene Douglas]. This time he'll keep coming and coming and coming."

And come he did. He wore down Skip Away by one length, giving Lukas a victory in seven of the last eight Triple Crown races and his tenth classic score.

• But Lukas' most profound comments came the morning after Grindstone's victory in the 1996 Kentucky Derby. Despite the joy he experienced from winning the

Derby, Lukas was still hurt over an article in the previous day's Louisville *Courier-Journal* in which several peers criticized him for being more of a marketer than a horseman. No one prided himself as a horseman more than Lukas. So, well before dawn and the media rush, Lukas poured his heart out to me, revealing a side to him that no one on the backstretch had ever seen.

"What did I ever do to deserve this?" he said. "The quotes they got were very unkind, and some of the people who were quoted swore to me they never said it. I really had to bite my tongue at the press conference in respect to Mr. Young [Grindstone's owner William T. Young]. I stand out here for four or five hours a day and try to do my job, and they've got me as some Barnum-and-Bailey guy that doesn't know a thing about a horse.

"I can't be somebody I'm not. Am I supposed to come here and wear a different type of clothes and change my whole makeup? I'm not supposed to be competent? I'm not supposed to be a good speaker? If a guy wants to put my name on a label of clothing, I should say 'no' because I'm a horse trainer? The quotes from the other trainers were very damaging, and I'm having trouble handling that. I've had an education and I've coached, so my background is different than a lot of horse trainers. I'm proud of my staff, and I'm proud of what we've done. That's what we are; deal with it. If that offends you, and you think I'm obnoxious, just say, 'I don't like that guy's personality.' But don't just keep hammering us all the time."

• Funny Cide's trainer, Barclay Tagg, on the pressure of having a horse going for the Triple Crown: "That's not pressure. You want to know what pressure is? Pressure is being flat broke with two kids in college and one horse left in your stable, and you've to haul it on a trailer to Penn National for the eleventh race on a snowy night. And if you don't get there, you're gonna be fired. Then you sit in the trailer with a blanket wrapped around you all night waiting for your race to come. That's pressure."

Despite his curmudgeonly persona, Tagg actually is one of the most refreshing people to talk to because he says what he feels, whether you like it or not, and is extremely protective of his horses. If Tagg wasn't complaining about something, he'd be miserable. He's one of my favorite people, and I love his comment to the media the morning before Funny Cide's attempt to sweep the Triple Crown in 2003.

"From twelve o'clock on Friday to Sunday morning, I'm not doing anything," he said. "Nobody's coming here. I'm going to have guards posted all around all night, and if you don't have a license saying you're employed by Barclay Tagg, you're not getting in here. I'm not going to church, so you can all come Sunday morning and criticize me or whatever you want to do. There won't be any victory party after the race. I'll just come back here to see if he's eaten his mash and then go home."

• No one watches the stretch run of a Triple Crown race quite like Nick Zito. And no one ever watched one in the frenzied manner Zito did at the 1994 Kentucky

Derby, won by Go for Gin.

As Go for Gin turned for home, having led almost every step of the way, Zito went into theatrics that were wild even for him. Where he comes up with them no one knows.

"You're a fighter, Gin; you're a fighter," he screamed through sandpaper-lined vocal cords. "We know the way ... we know the way ... we know the way. You're a fighter. One more furlong to go. Run for the roses as fast as you can."

As Go for Gin crossed the wire, Zito threw a kiss to heavens. "I love you, God. I love you. I love you. We know the way."

He then charged the ABC camera and stuck his face up against it, as if he were about to devour it. Having worked himself into a state of near delirium, he concluded his verbal eruption.

"I love you, America. I love my kids. I love everybody."

• If there was one celebrity that provided racing with its biggest shot in the arm it was actor Jack Klugman, of *The Odd Couple* and *Quincy* fame. Klugman was a true lover of the sport and betting. He even devoted an entire episode of *The Odd Couple* to horse racing, filming it at Belmont Park.

In 1980, Klugman, who had owned horses on and off for years, not only had his first top-class colt, he made it to the Kentucky Derby. The horse, a gray named Jaklin Klugman (yes, it was a Jockey Club error) came to Churchill Downs with a legitimate shot to win the Run for the Roses. The day before the race Klugman discussed just what this horse meant to him.

"I've always been a workaholic," he said. "All that mattered outside my family was work, work, work. I was getting jaded; the same thing over and over again. Then this horse came along, and I fell in love with him. He wouldn't marry me, but I love him. He gave me somewhere to go. He gave me an outlet that's so exciting. I bought a place and turned it into a horse farm, and I'm going to live with the horses six months out of the year. I already have three broodmares, so look out Spendthrift Farm.

"You don't really know about something until it comes along. I remember the old comic Joe E. Lewis. He had a piano player for twenty years, and he said about him, 'I never knew he drank until he came in sober one day.' That's the way it is with the horses. You never know how much you love them until someone says, 'Hey, look how terrific it can be.' "

• In January 2006, I called trainer Michael Matz for a small "Derby Watch" feature I was writing on Barbaro, who was undefeated but had never run on dirt. I asked him if he knew where Barbaro's name came from. He called out to his assistant, Peter Brette, and asked, "Hey, Peter, what does the name Barbaro mean?"

Brette didn't hesitate with his answer: "Kentucky Derby winner."

"In our dreams, right?" Matz replied.

Well, dreams obviously do come true.

Photo Credits

Page 1: Spectacular Bid with Davona Dale (Steve Haskin); Spectacular Bid after the Preakness (The Blood-Horse); Bud Delp (Milt Toby)

Page 2: 1985 Kentucky Derby first turn (Dan Johnson); Angel Cordero and his wife Margie (Barbara D. Livingston)

Page 3: Strodes Creek (Barbara D. Livingston); Charlie Whittingham and Sunday Silence (Candace Rushing)

Page 4: Arazi arrives at Churchill Downs (Barbara D. Livingston); Arazi followed by the media (Barbara D. Livingston); Prairie Bayou with Mike Smith (Barbara D. Livingston)

Page 5: Irgun (Barbara D. Livingston); Unbridled's Song (Barbara D. Livingston); Unbridled's Song's foot problems (Barbara D. Livingston)

Page 6: Louis Quatorze Preakness (Tim Herman); Nick Zito with Steve Haskin at Preakness (Skip Dickstein)

Page 7: Touch Gold and trainer David Hofmans (Barbara D. Livingston); Silver Charm to Belmont paddock (Anne M. Eberhardt); Touch Gold wins Belmont (Rick Samuels)

Page 8: Captain Steve Thompson and Mike Pegram at Churchill Downs (Anne M. Eberhardt); Derby winner Real Quiet with Pegram and trainer Bob Baffert (Steve Haskin); Charismatic wins the Derby (Barbara D. Livingston); Charismatic's lucky connections (Anne M. Eberhardt)

Page 9: Fusaichi Pegasus with trainer Neil Drysdale and exercise rider Andy Durnin (Skip Dickstein); trainer Eddie Gregson (Benoit); Fusaichi Pegasus (Barbara D. Livingston)

Page 10: Trainer John Ward greets Jorge Chavez and Monarchos (Skip Dickstein); Yvonne Azeff, Bryan Beccia, and Tammy Holz with Monarchos' Derby walkover (The Blood-Horse)

Page 11: Trainer Nancy Alberts saddles Magic Weisner for Preakness (Barbara D. Livingston); Magic Weisner and War Emblem in Preakness (Skip Dickstein)

Page 12: Sarava wins Belmont (Alexander Barkoff); Bob Baffert with Mike Jenner on War Emblem (Mark Cornelison/Lexington Herald-Leader); Sarava and Hanne Jorgensen (Barbara D. Livingston)

Page 13: Van carrying Smarty Jones to Belmont (Bill Denver/ Equi-Photo); Smarty Jones' Kentucky Derby win (Barbara D. Livingston); Smarty Jones at Philadelpia Park (Barbara D. Livingston)

Page 14: Afleet Alex's Preakness stumble (Horsephotos/NTRA); Afleet Alex wins Belmont (Barbara D. Livingston)

Pages 15: Barbaro at Fair Hill (Barbara D. Livingston); Barbaro's Derby win (Barbara D. Livingston)

Page 16: Arts and Letters (The Blood-Horse); Stage Door Johnny (Winants Brothers); Jim French with trainer John Campo (Paul Schafer/NYRA)

Cover Photos: Touch Gold's Belmont victory (Rick Samuels); Sunday Silence's and Easy Goer's Preakness battle (Skip Dickstein); Monarchos' Derby win (Barbara D. Livingston); Steve Haskin with Strodes Creek (courtesy of Steve Haskin)

About the Author

Steve Haskin

S teve Haskin is the award-winning senior correspondent for *The Blood-Horse*, the leading Thoroughbred industry weekly. Haskin, who spent twenty-nine years with *Daily Racing Form* before joining *The Blood-Horse*, is known for his insightful coverage of the Triple Crown races.

Haskin has written a number of books, including *Horse Racing's Holy Grail: The Epic Quest for the Kentucky Derby* and *Baffert: Dirt Road to the Derby* as well as biographies of John Henry, Dr. Fager, and Kelso for the Thoroughbred Legends series. He lives in Hamilton Square, New Jersey.